NORDHAUSEN
CONCENTRATION CAMP

THEN AND NOW

NORDHAUSEN
CONCENTRATION CAMP
THEN AND NOW

Karel Margry

AFTER THE BATTLE

An Imprint of Pen & Sword Books Ltd

Nordhausen Concentration Camp Then and Now

Published by After the Battle
An imprint of Pen & Sword Books Ltd
47 Church Street, Barnsley,
South Yorkshire, S70 2AS
Tel. 01226 734222
Fax. 01226 734438
Email: enquiries@pen-and-sword.co.uk
Website: **www.afterthebattle.com**
www.pen-and-sword.co.uk

Printed and bound in India by Replika Press Pvt. Ltd.

ISBN: 9781399031219

Commissioning Editor: Rob Green
Editor: Karel Margry
Design: Paul Wilkinson

Credits:
The two chapters of this book were earlier published as articles in *After the Battle* magazine:
'Nordhausen' in issue 101 (November 1998);
'The Gardelegen Massacre' in issue 111 (May 2001).

Acknowledgements:
The author would like to thank Dr. Kornelia Klose, Torsten Hess and Christine Janischefski of the Gedenkstätte Mittelbau-Dora; Manfred Bornemann and Fred Dittmann for permission to use the excellent maps drawn by them, and Percy Upton for the loan of photographs. Special thanks go to Alvin Gilens for permission to use his photos taken inside the Kohnstein mountain. The author further thanks Dr Herbert Becker, former director of the Gardelegen Stadtmuseum and of the Mahn- und Gedenkstätte Gardelegen, and Dipl.-Hist. Wally Schulz, former director of the Stadtmuseum. The Gardelegen story is primarily based on the US War Crimes Investigation Team file on the Gardelegen case, an original copy of which is held at the Nederlands Instituut voor Oorlogsdocumentatie in Amsterdam.

Photo Credit Abbreviations:
BA – Bundesarchiv; IWM – Imperial War Museum; NIOD – Nederlands Instituut voor Oorlogsdocumentatie, Amsterdam; USNA – US National Archives. Unless specified otherwise, all illustrations are from the *After the Battle* archive.

Front Cover: A freed Polish inmate of concentration camp 'Dora' at Nordhausen shows one of the ovens in the camp crematorium to Tech/5 John L. Lyndon of the US Army on April 14, 1945, three days after the camp's liberation by American forces – then and now. (USNA/Karel Margry)

Back Cover:
Top left: A V2 rocket on the production line of the Mittelwerk underground factory inside the Kohnstein mountain at Nordhausen pictured in April 1945 – and a rusted V2 engine on display in the same tunnels today. (USNA/Karel Margry)

Top right: The Isenschnibbe barn outside the town of Gardelegen, site of the mass murder of 1,016 prisoners from 'Dora' and from Hannover-Stöcken on April 13, 1945 – then and now. (USNA/Karel Margry)

Bottom: The cemetery of honour for the victims of the Gardelegen massacre. (Karel Margry)

CONTENTS

INTRODUCTION

IN THE HISTORY OF NAZI concentration camps, and particularly labour camps, there is probably no place that bears the same stigma of wretchedness as 'Dora-Mittelbau' at Nordhausen. Located in the Harz mountains in central Germany, next to a quarry tunnel system in the Kohnstein mountain, it served to house thousands of slave workers for an underground factory known as the 'Mittelwerk', which produced three of Germany's best-known secret weapons: the V1 flying bomb, the V2 rocket and engines for the Messerschmitt Me 262 and Arado Ar 234 jet fighters. With over 20 kilometres of underground galleries, it was the largest underground factory in the world. Many of the slave labourers died in indescribable misery, being forced to extend the tunnels with meagre equipment and under ghastly conditions, sometimes not seeing daylight for weeks on end.

Started in August 1943, 'Mittelbau-Dora' in due course became the centre of a whole complex of underground factories in the Nordhausen area, with several subsidiary camps being set up. In all, of some 60,000 prisoners sent there between 1943 and 1945, 20,000 were driven to extinction to implement Nazi Germany's secret weapons programme, but they laboured late and in vain, for the products they yielded had little impact on the war. The V1 and V2 are the only weapons which cost more lives in production than in deployment: far more people died producing them than were killed by their explosive impact in London, Antwerp and elsewhere.

Originally, camp 'Dora', where most of the slave labourers for the secret factory were housed, was an Aussenlager (sub-camp) of Buchenwald concentration camp. However, on October 1, 1944, to reflect its growing importance for the German war effort, its status was changed to that of an independent Hauptlager (Main Camp), the smaller camps in the region becoming its Aussenlager. Thus 'Dora' obtained a status on a par with Nazi Germany's other main camps Dachau, Sachsenhausen, Buchenwald, Flossenbürg, Mauthausen, Neuengamme, Gross-Rosen, Ravensbrück, Auschwitz, Natzweiler, Majdanek, Stutthof and Bergen-Belsen.

The history of Nordhausen, already gruesome in itself, ended in a crescendo of violence when, in the final weeks of the war, the surviving inmates were evacuated from the camps in 'death marches'. One group of over a thousand men then became victim of one of the most horrendous of all Nazi atrocities. On April 13, 1945, just outside the town of Gardelegen, their SS camp guards, helped by local troops and Hitlerjugend, locked the prisoners in a big barn and set fire to the inside, burning those inside, killing them with hand-grenades, and shooting anyone who tried to escape from the burning, smoke-filled building. A total of 1,016 men died as a result. When discovered by American troops two days later, Gardelegen quickly became known as the site of one most notorious war crimes committed by the Nazis.

This book recounts the history of Nordhausen concentration camp and of the Gardelegen massacre in full detail. Both stories are illustrated with unique Then and Now comparison photographs.

Karel Margry,
September 2023.

Supervised by US Army soldiers, German civilians bury dead from the Nordhausen camp in mass graves in a field opposite the town cemetery on April 14, 1945. (USNA)

NORDHAUSEN CONCENTRATION CAMP

WHEN IN AUGUST 1943, the German rocket development centre at Peenemünde on the Baltic coast was destroyed by British bombers, the transfer of V2 rocket series production to underground factories became acute. However, the decision to go underground had already been taken earlier.

Ten months before, on October 3, 1942, the V2 (also known as Aggregat 4, or A4) had made its first successful launch at the Heeresversuchsanstalt (HVA, Army Experimental Station) Peenemünde. On December 22, Hitler

The Kohnstein mountain near Nordhausen in central Germany where the Nazi regime in 1943 installed the 'Mittelwerk' underground factory, which produced three of Germany's best-known secret weapons: the V1 flying bomb, the V2 rocket and engines for the Me 262 and Ar 234 jet fighters. A gypsum quarry had been established in the Kohnstein in the late 19th century, and decades of open-air mining had already radically altered its shape by the time the secret underground factory moved in in 1943. This is how the mountain looked from the south in early 1945. Niedersachswerfen is on the right, and the southern entrances to the tunnel system and Lager 'Dora', the concentration camp housing the slave workers for the factory, can be seen below the tree line on the far left. (This picture was taken by the British scientific research team which surveyed the Mittelwerk after its capture by the Allies in April 1945.) (BA)

approved a plan submitted by Albert Speer, his Minister for Armament and Ammunition, for the setting up of an experimental series production of 500 V2s to be produced at Peenemünde and at the Zeppelin works at Friedrichshafen. On January 15, 1943, Speer appointed Gerhard Degenkolb, an energetic manager who had proved his mettle in locomotive production, to head a Sonder-Ausschuss A4 (A4 Special Committee) to carry out this order.

Within his Special Committee, Degenkolb created several 'working committees', each charged with taking care of a specific part of the task at

The photographer stood just outside the hamlet of Krimderode, about halfway between Nordhausen and the mountain, near where the village road crosses the Harz-Querbahn (the narrow-gauge railway which runs right across the Harz mountains from Nordhausen 60 kilometres north to Wernigerode). Note that the mountain has seen spectacular further changes in the decades since 1945, the entire eastern (right) half having now fallen victim to continued quarrying. (Karel Margry)

hand, and coordinating the efforts of the Peenemünde technicians and the supply industry. There were seven logistical and supply committees: Raw Materials, Oxygen, Workforce, Deliveries, Transport, Building Projects, and Installations & Assets; two rocket technical committees: Fuselages and Electrical Equipment; and one Production Planning committee. The latter,

The Kohnstein mountain lies three kilometres north-west of Nordhausen, and is actually closer to the village of Niedersachswerfen, which lies along its eastern face.

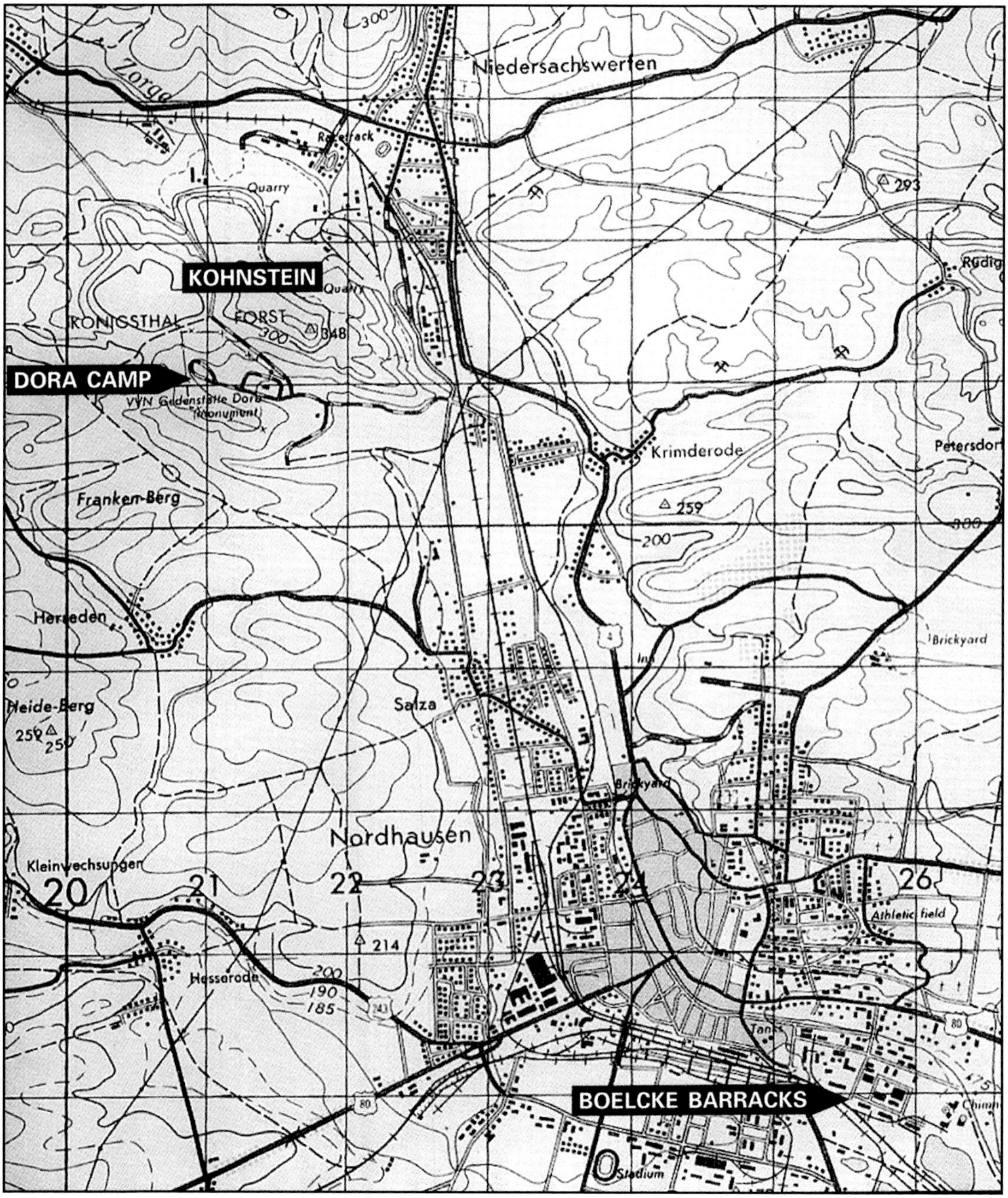

led by Detmar Stahlknecht, was based at Peenemünde, Raw Materials was in the Ruhr area, all others had their headquarters in Berlin.

Oberst Walter Dornberger, the chief of the Rocket Development Section in the Heereswaffenamt (Army Ordnance Department) who had led the Army's rocket programme since 1933, soon grew unhappy with the new set-up as he thought the rocket production could best remain under complete Army control and, furthermore, could only succeed if given a top priority status. But he had no choice but to go along.

In April, Degenkolb raised the V2 production target from 600 a month at two production sites (Stahlknecht Programme) to 900 a month in three places: at Peenemünde, at Friedrichshafen, and at the Rax locomotive factories in Wiener-Neustadt (Degenkolb Programme). The reason for spreading production was to make it less vulnerable to air attacks, but Degenkolb already realised that the best solution was to create underground factories. Feverishly, his Special Committee, the Heereswaffenamt and the HVA Peenemünde began scouting Germany and occupied Europe for a suitable site for such a factory. The risk of above-ground production was brought home on June 22, when the RAF bombed the Friedrichshafen works, paralysing V2 production there.

Two days before, on June 20, Hitler had stipulated to Speer that the V2 programme was now more urgent than all other armament programmes, a top priority which was confirmed after Dornberger (newly promoted to Generalmajor) and his chief engineer, Wernher von Braun, had presented the new weapon in a personal interview with Hitler at the Wolfsschanze FHQ on July 7. Finally, all industrial resources of the Reich would become available for rocket production.

Until now, rockets had been a concern of the armed forces and the armaments ministry. However, on July 10, Reichsführer-SS Heinrich Himmler, who for a long time had been looking for an opportunity to get a finger into the rocket programme, convinced Hitler that he should be put in charge of security against espionage and sabotage of the V2 project. It was the first step in a development that would eventually give the SS complete control of the whole rocket programme.

THE WIFO COMPLEX IN THE KOHNSTEIN MOUNTAIN

Meanwhile, the search for underground facilities continued. Then, around the middle of July, Paul Figge, chief of the Deliveries Committee, heard in Kassel about a giant underground oil depot in the Kohnstein mountain at Niedersachswerfen near Nordhausen in the southern Harz region in central Germany. Figge at once travelled to Nordhausen to inspect the facilities, and immediately saw that it was exactly what the rocket planners had been looking for.

Lying north-west of Nordhausen and west of Niedersachswerfen and rising steeply from the countryside, the Kohnstein is composed almost

What later became the V-weapon underground factory was initially designed as a secret storage facility for Germany's strategic oil and lubricants reserve. Planning on the ladder-shaped complex was begun in 1934 by a state-controlled company named the Wirtschaftliche Forschungsgesellschaft (Wifo), and tunnelling proceeded in three phases. The first phase (1936-37) saw completion of the first 18 galleries; the second (1937-40) brought it as deep as Gallery 42; and the third (1941-43) had only reached Gallery 45 when, in July 1943, the Wifo was forced to evacuate the fuel depot to make room for production of the V2. (Map by Manfred Bornemann)

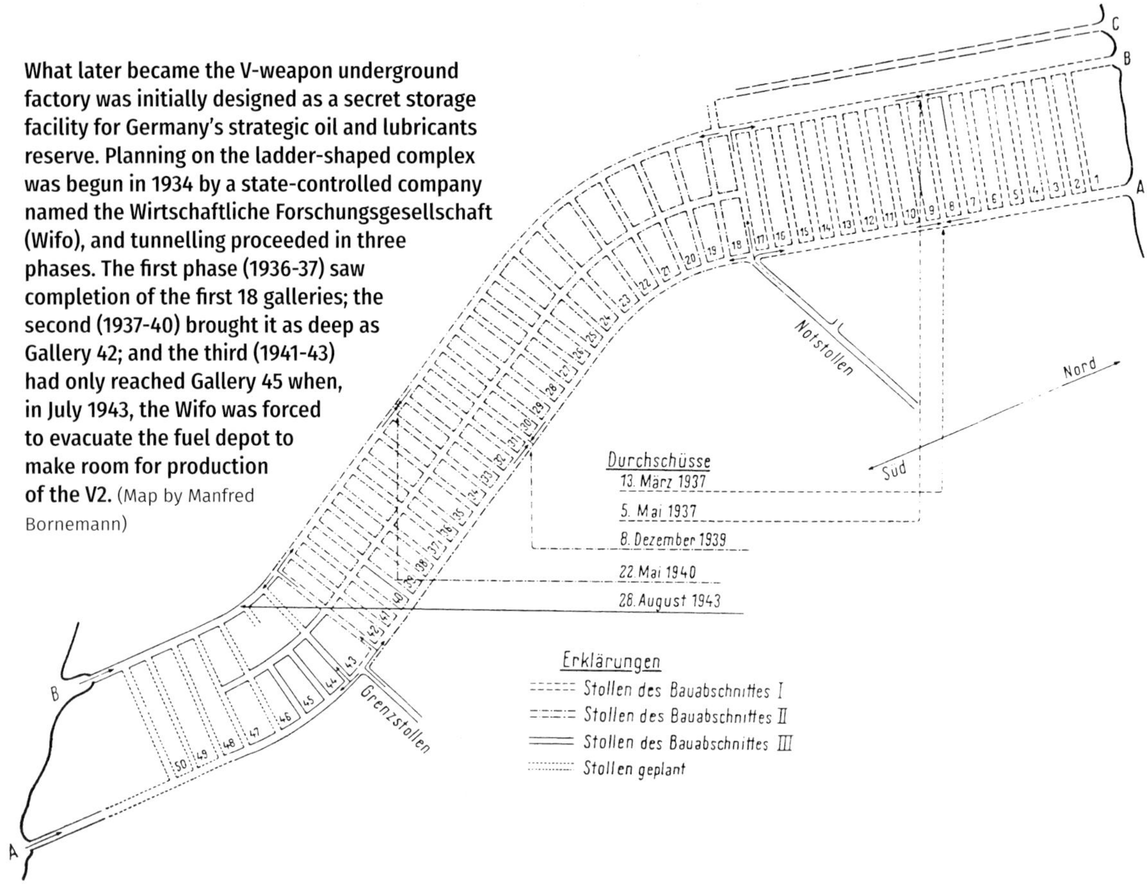

Because today the memory of Mittelbau-Dora is kept alive at the southern end of the Kohnstein, people tend to forget that the tunnel complex was initially begun at the northern side. This is the northern entrance to Tunnel A.

(Gedenkstätte Mittelbau-Dora)

…alcium sulphite), soft stone
…orthern and eastern sides,
…top of the limestone lies a
… is covered by loam. Several
…ohnsteinkopf (332m), Hoher
…f (300m). Three valleys – the
…flanks.

…ppeared under a wall of waste stone dumped here by the

The first tunnel to run all the way through the mountain was Tunnel B, and it was only pushed through on August 28, 1943 – just when the Wifo fuel depot was moving out and the Mittelwerk V2 factory moving in. It then became the tunnel where the V2 production line (which ran from north to south) was set up. This is how the southern entrance of Tunnel B looked at the end of the war. (The railway points in the foreground help to differentiate this tunnel from Tunnel A – compare with the plan on pages 28-29). Camouflage has been put up to hide the tunnel from observation from the air. The small hut on the right was the sick bay for the slave workers in the early months of the Mittelwerk, at the time when these unfortunates were working (and living) underground and before the camp hospital was ready. Note the watchtowers on the slope above. (USNA)

Blown up by the Soviet Army in 1948, this is what the southern entrance to Tunnel B looks like today. (Karel Margry)

Quarrying at the Kohnstein had begun as early as the 1870s. Gypsum is a prime component for the production of synthetic ammonia, which itself is a prime component for the production of nitrogenous fertilizer and, more important in wartime, nitrogenous explosive. In 1916-17, the Badische Anilin- & Soda-Fabrik established a gypsum factory at Niedersachswerfen to supply its newly-built ammonia factory at Merseburg. Open-cast mining was begun, deliveries being some 32,000 tons in 1918, rising to 82,000 the following year.

After World War I, with the complete fusion of the eight major paint-producing factories in Germany into the huge IG Farben GmbH in 1925, the Gipswerk Niedersachswerfen factory became part of that concern. Production rose steadily, reaching 1,244,000 tons in 1928, but dropping dramatically after 1930 to about a third of that as a result of the economic depression. The quarry never regained the high production volumes of the 1920s, for ammonia-based fertilizers were increasingly replaced by other types of fertilizers. By 1935, some 11 million tons of lime and gypsum, and two million tons of waste, had been mined, representing a total of 4.3 million cubic metres of earth moved. The waste had been dumped in the Gängertal, completely filling up the valley and changing the north-eastern face of the Kohnstein massif.

In 1934, one year after the Nazis came to power, the IG Farben and the Deutsche Gesellschaft für öffentliche Arbeiten (German Company for Public Works – an organisation of the Ministry of Economics) jointly founded the Wirtschaftliche Forschungsgesellschaft (Wifo, Economic Research Company) as an organisation to secure the supply of strategic raw materials in case of war. One of its projects was the creation of an underground central fuel depot (Zentrales Kraftstoff-Lager). Looking for a suitable site, the IG Farben proposed to the Wifo to dig tunnels into the Kohnstein. The geological conditions made tunnelling easy, the site was well connected to the German traffic system, and the project was financially advantageous to both parties: sharing the cost of tunnelling, the Merseburg factory would get its lime cheap, and the Wifo its underground depot at a lower cost. The new depot was named the Wifo-Aussenstelle (sub-works) Niedersachswerfen.

All that existed at that time at the Kohnstein quarry was an emergency gallery (Not-Stollen) and a boundary gallery (Grenz-Stollen) further east. Initial Wifo plans called for two galleries to be dug parallel, with a single storage gallery to connect the two. In August 1936, the Wifo engineer appointed to direct the project, Karl Wilhelm Neu, proposed a much larger scheme: to deepen the two parallel tunnels enough to create 18 connecting galleries – the tunnels would serve as transport roads, the galleries as the fuel storage rooms. Digging would proceed from two directions, both from the tunnel entrances and from the deep end of the emergency gallery.

Work began in June 1936. Using a work-force of 400 miners, it progressed smoothly, the eastern main gallery (Tunnel A) being shot through on March 13, 1937, and the western one (Tunnel B) on May 5. Lateral galleries were

Although its southern entrance was already begun in 1941, Tunnel A was not finally opened all the way through until January 1944, the last 300 or so metres having been dug, under indescribable misery and hardship and virtually with their bare hands, by concentration camp slaves. After August 1944, this end of Tunnel A became the exit for the V1 factory which had been set up in the galleries closest to it, Nos. 43-47. This explains the pile of typical V1 wire-wound compressed-air bottles on the left, and the wooden V1 trolley in the foreground. (USNA)

Like its twin, Tunnel A was closed by demolition by the Soviets in 1948. (Karel Margry)

The monastery buildings at Ilfeld, five kilometres north of the Kohnstein, where both the A4 Special Committee and the Mittelwerk company set up their headquarters. (Karel Margry)

blown through as the tunnels proceeded. All galleries were rectangular, nine metres wide and seven metres high. In all, 260,000 cubic metres of stone (780,000 tons of limestone) were removed.

To preclude condensation, it proved necessary to install ventilation equipment. Fresh air from three ventilation shafts was first dried in a six-furnace central heating installed in Gallery 1 before being blown into the tunnels. An air outlet shaft was installed at the deep end. On completion, Galleries 2-18 soon became filled with thousands of oil drums containing the fuel reserve of the Third Reich.

A double-track railway was built into the tunnels to connect the fuel depot with the main rail system. To create office space and housing for its personnel, the Wifo built a small settlement of two office blocks and, by 1943, 20 houses just outside Niedersachswerfen. Another Wifo project at Niedersachswerfen was a cement factory, built in 1940 on the east side of the Kohnstein, between the mountain and the main railway.

Even before the drum depot (Wifo I) was ready, plans were made to extend the tunnel complex right through to the southern end of the mountain. The two parallel main tunnels, both some 1,800 metres long and running in a soft 'S' form, would have a total of 50 lateral galleries, each between 150-200 metres long. Instead of the stacks of oil drums in Galleries 2-18, the new galleries would each hold two huge 80-metre-long oil containers, each with a capacity of one million litres. To encompass the tanks, the galleries would be circular, with a diameter of 11 metres.

The extension proceeded in two phases, named Wifo II and Wifo III.

Another part dug by the slave prisoners was Gallery 46 or, to be more exact, the eastern half of it (the western half was never begun). This was one of the four galleries (Nos. 43-46) used, between October 1943 and June 1944, as living quarters for the prisoners – where thousands squatted in semi-darkness in overcrowded, four-tiered bunks which reached as high as the ceiling, and scenes of unimaginable suffering and dying took place. Later, Gallery 46 became one the five where V1 series production took place. Today, it is one of those that can be viewed by visitors of the Mittelbau-Dora Memorial. (Karel Margry)

Wifo II brought the tunnels as far as Gallery 42. Again, digging proceeded from two directions – in the north from the emergency gallery opposite Gallery 17, and in the south from the boundary gallery which hit Tunnel A between the planned Galleries 42 and 43. Tunnel A was blown through on December 8, 1939, and B on May 22, 1940. From Gallery 17 to 42, a third tunnel, running between and parallel with A and B, was built to serve as service gallery for the oil tanks. In all, 700,000 cubic metres of stone (2.1 million tons of lime) were removed.

The final stretch, Wifo III, proved to be the most difficult. The geological composition at the southern end of the Kohnstein made the risk of collapse much greater, and the Wifo had to call in a specialist firm to do the work. Tunnelling could now only proceed using scaffolding and wood lining, and galleries had to be secured with concrete walls. They would have a vaulted profile of nine metres wide and six-and-a-half metres high. Because of the risk, it was decided to begin with completing one tunnel, Tunnel B, again digging from two sides. It was a slow and dangerous process. Work began in July 1941 and it took two years before the tunnel was finally shot through, on August 28, 1943. Now, Tunnel B ran all the way through the mountain, with entrances on both sides.

By then, Tunnel A had progressed as far as Gallery 45; a southern entrance for it had been begun; the service tunnel running parallel with A and B had advanced as far as Gallery 47; and the eastern half of Galleries 43-45 been completed. Of the 42 galleries, Nos. 2 to 16 contained some 15,000 tons of oil and lubricants in barrels (i.e. over 15 million litres); two huge tanks, each containing one million litres of hydrogen-superoxide, had been installed in Gallery 17. Further into the tunnel, the central part was reserved for war chemicals, the southern part for petrol. Even in its half-finished state, it was the largest fuel depot in Germany, estimated to cover the wartime needs of all three services for two years.

THE 'MITTELWERK' COMPANY

This then was the situation when Paul Figge discovered the Wifo complex in July 1943. (The man who had first told him about it was probably company director Paul Radtke of the Nordhausen steel firm of MABAG; Radtke was a member of the Armaments Committee in Berlin and he knew the Wifo depot because his firm had installed the underframes for the oil drums there.) Soon after, Figge brought Degenkolb and his executive Heinz Kunze to see for themselves. Shortly after, Dornberger also inspected the site. At first, both the Armaments Ministry and the Heereswaffenamt independently tried to take over the depot for rocket production, Speer's ministry even going so far as to attempt to completely buy up the Wifo. The Wifo resisted strongly, pointing out the strategic importance of the fuel depot. They enlisted Reichsmarschall Hermann Göring who, in his capacity as President of the Reich Research Council, intervened willingly on their behalf, because he was jealous of the priority which Speer's projects got over those of the Luftwaffe.

However, in late July, Hitler decided that the Wifo was to evacuate the depot and that the tunnel complex be made available for V2 production. A contract was soon negotiated, the Armaments Ministry renting the complex for 1 million Reichsmark a month (later lowered to 500,000 Reichsmark), and taking over equipment and personnel at a fixed price per day.

To organise the move to Nordhausen and set up the production line there, Degenkolb created two new working committees: Transfer (a subordinate of Figge's Deliveries Committee), and Series Production, the latter led by Albin Sawatzki, an engineer from the Henschel transportation equipment works who had proved his worth in series production of the Tiger tank.

That same month, July 1943, Karl Otto Saur, leader of the Technical Department in Speer's ministry and Degenkolb's chief, suddenly and to everyone's consternation announced that instead of Degenkolb's plan to produce 900 V2s a month, the target would be raised to 2,000 a month to be produced at Peenemünde, Friedrichshafen, Wiener-Neustadt and Nordhausen (Saur Programme). In addition, he wanted a monthly production of 20,000 to 25,000 V1 flying bombs (officially known as the Fi 103). All involved judged this plan far too ambitious.

However, this grandiose scheme was soon overtaken by events. On August 13, American bombers severely damaged the Rax works at Wiener-Neustadt (they were to have bombed the nearby Messerschmitt aircraft factories, but hit the more conspicuous Rax buildings instead). Five days later, on the night of August 17/18, the RAF hit Peenemünde. Although neither the V2 development section nor the V2 assembly lines (where series production was planned to start in September) were decisively hit, the raid made clear that the enemy had discovered the secret of Peenemünde. With all three above-ground production sites now bombed, and probably kept under close surveillance by the enemy, the move to underground factories had become a matter of utmost urgency.

On August 19, one day after the Peenemünde raid, Speer reported to Hitler at his Wolfsschanze FHQ to report on the damage done by the raid and discuss plans to move production to Nordhausen. The conferences on this lasted until the 22nd. Himmler and Saur were present and when Speer mentioned that a major handicap was the lack of sufficient labour to set up the underground factory, Himmler saw his chance to really get into the V2 programme. He offered to supply the workforce from concentration camp inmates, and to use them both to get the underground factory ready in minimum time and for series production itself. He guaranteed complete secrecy since the prisoners would be completely shut off from all contact with the outside world. Hitler approved.

Efforts between the A4 Special Committee and the SS-Wirtschafts- und Verwaltungshauptamt (WVHA, SS Main Department for Economic Administration – the authority administering the concentration camps) were quickly coordinated. Degenkolb charged SS-Brigadeführer Hans Kammler, the young and ruthless chief of the WVHA's Amtsgruppe C (Building Construction), with carrying out the order. Already on August 27, just one week after Hitler's decision, the first group of 107 camp inmates was sent from Buchenwald concentration camp to Nordhausen, followed by a second of 1,223 on September 2.

On September 21, within a month of the FHQ conference, Speer's ministry (newly renamed the Reich Ministry for Armament and War Production), and Kammler formally founded the Mittelwerk GmbH (Central Works Ltd) as the company running the underground factory. Appointed managing director was Dr Kurt Kettler who, like Degenkolb, had made his name in locomotive production.

The contract signed between the Wifo and the Mittelwerk on September 6 stipulated that the actual work, i.e. the completion of the underground facilities, would continue to be directed by the Wifo staff, since they already possessed the technical knowledge and experience for this specialist work, and using the same civil industrial and mining firms. The only change was that the orders would now come from the Mittelwerk GmbH, and that the majority of the work-force would now be composed of concentration camp inmates. The jobs at hand were: completion of the Wifo phase III tunnels;

removal of the Wifo dump from the Kohnstein; transformation of the tunnel complex to a production-line factory; construction of road and railway connections, and building of a hutted camp for the labour force.

Detailed plans were drawn up listing exact requirements for the factory as regards electrical power, heating, ventilation, supply of water and compressed air; the precise division of the 97,400 square metres of underground floor space and the specific function assigned to each underground gallery; and the number of workers needed (planned at 2,000 Germans and 16,000 slave workers).

The actual V2 assembly line, 1,502 metres long, would be set up in Tunnel B, with component parts being produced in workshops installed in the side galleries. Tunnel A would serve as supply street for the workshops and factory, a roadway and a double-track railway traversing the whole length of the tunnel.

Though both were huge operations in every aspect, the transfer to the new location, and the new underground factory itself were to be kept totally secret, and so a large number of code-names, false addresses and nondescript field post numbers were created to conceal the location and purpose of the new factory. The company name 'Mittelwerk' (Central Works) reflected the factory's location in central Germany (there were also plans for a Nordwerk and an Ostwerk), but did not give a clue as to its activities. The company's mail went via a post office box at Halle an der Saale, 100 kilometres distant. 'Mittelraum' was the code-name given to the area around Nordhausen where the company deployed its activities. 'Mittelbau' was the term for the construction projects undertaken in the Mittelraum (in time, it also came to be used as an alternative to Mittelraum, i.e. a geographical designation). 'Dora' was the name for the main camp housing the slave labourers for the Mittelraum projects. In charge of security measures, and also appointed camp commander of 'Dora', was SS-Sturmbannführer Otto Förschner (as of October 5, he was also nominated Mittelwerk managing director on a par with Kettler).

On August 21, Hitler had stipulated that the three original V2 factories should continue to produce rockets while the underground factory was being built up; the target was to manufacture 900 a month above-ground and 900 underground. Then, in early September, he changed his mind and decided that all 1,800 should be produced at Nordhausen. All personnel and machines of the other factories were to be transferred to Nordhausen forthwith so as to speed up completion of the factory there. However, on October 8, at a conference between the Heereswaffenamt, the A4 Special Committee and the Mittelwerk, the production target was lowered to the much more realistic figure of 900 a month, and this was the figure mentioned in the top-secret formal rocket production order issued by the Oberkommando des Heeres (OKH, Army High Command) on October 19. The OKH order commissioned the Mittelwerk to produce a total of 12,000 rockets, with a monthly delivery of 900 at 40,000 Reichsmark a piece (total price 480 million Reichsmark). By the same order, the Mittelwerk took over all the rights, obligations, and outstanding orders of the factories which had been involved in rocket production until then. (In the autumn of 1944, the Mittelwerk would also formally absorb the Wifo-Aussenstelle.) Although the precise financial details remained to be worked out, this did not hamper the start of production, both because of the project's top priority and because the Armaments Ministry guaranteed payments.

One by one, the various organisations involved moved to the Nordhausen area. First to open office, on September 1, in a hut next to the tunnel entrance, was Sawatzki's Series Production Committee (Sawatzki was nominated the Mittelwerk's Technical Director). Other committees found space in requisitioned inns and cafes in Niedersachswerfen and Wernigerode. The Mittelwerk commercial section took over the offices of the Wifo housing settlement. The former monastery complex at Ilfeld, just five kilometres to the north, which since 1940 had housed the Napola (National Socialist Cadre School) Ilfeld, was taken over to become the Mittelwerk company headquarters and seat of the A4 Special Committee. The huge complex also served as billets and reception centre for German civilian personnel. (In early 1944, the Special Committee would move to Rübeland in the central Harz, the commercial section moving to take over its offices at Ilfeld.)

CAMP 'DORA'

However, little care was given to accommodating the slave labourers. As long as the hutted camp was not yet ready, they were to live in the underground complex itself, deep inside the mountain – which meant that those inmates assigned to work in the tunnels would not get to see any daylight at all, and this sometimes for weeks on end. At first, the prisoners were assigned to Gallery 39, a room covering an area of 1,800 square metres. All they were given were a few carbide lamps, latrine buckets, and straw and blankets to sleep on. From October, a prisoner carpentry squad was ordered to build multi-storied wooden bunks in the newly-shot-through Galleries 43 to 46. With some 6,000 prisoners cramped into them, these four rooms – 120 metres long by 12 metres wide and 9 metres high; dark, damp, cold, and separated from the main tunnels by wooden and canvas walls – became a veritable hell on earth. Even with men from night and day shifts alternating a bunk, there was not nearly enough space for everyone. The three- and four-storied bunks could hardly carry the weight and sometimes collapsed, killing many inmates. The only lighting came from weak lamps hung widely apart. Beyond Gallery 18 no ventilation, water or heating had yet been installed, and the atmosphere in the galleries was decidedly unhealthy. Every explosion set off by the tunnellers at work almost next-door filled the whole rooms with a blinding, suffocating dust. Sanitation was catastrophic. The prisoners had to use improvised latrines, made up of halved oil drums with a plank on top. Set up in Tunnel A in alcoves opposite the galleries,

Simultaneously with the work on the tunnels, the slave workers had to build their own concentration camp on the southern slopes of the Kohnstein. Named 'Dora', it was originally a sub-camp of Buchenwald, but in October 1944 it became an independent main camp. 'Dora' was the last of the large concentration camps created by Nazi Germany. The early camps built in the 1930s, like Dachau, Buchenwald or Sachsenhausen, were all given big, stone gate-buildings, all of similar design and meant to impress both inmates and public opinion. However, by 1943, the SS no longer bothered about these, and camps like Belsen and 'Dora' were built without one. Moreover, 'Dora' was a totally secret camp, not meant to be seen by anyone not involved in the Mittelwerk project, so there was no need for an imposing gatehouse. Its entrance was merely flanked by two wooden huts, the one seen here (Block 29) housing the Gestapo section, and the one opposite (Block 1) the SS camp administration. (Gedenkstätte Mittelbau-Dora)

Today, only the rail track – which connected the camp with the nearby goods-train station – remains. (Karel Margry)

The camp as seen from the southern slope of the valley in which it lay. The two gate huts seen in the previous picture are on the far right, with the Appellplatz (roll-call square) adjoining them, and the various camp blocks stretching out to the left. The low building visible in the right foreground is the camp prison. The crematorium can be seen hidden in the woods on the far slope on the left. (Gedenkstätte Mittelbau-Dora)

The same panorama today. (Karel Margry)

they filled the deeper tunnels with a terrible stench and were a source of deadly infections. Every evening, a prisoner squad had to load the barrels on train wagons and empty them outside. There was no washing or drinking water, and prisoners quenched their thirst with moist on the walls or water lapped up from mud; some used urine to wash the dust off their bodies. As food, the prisoners only received Ersatz coffee and bread, with an occasional slice of sausage or margarine added to it, in the morning and thin soup in the afternoon and evening. Dysentery, tuberculosis and other diseases ran rampant.

The work itself was exhausting and dangerous. Driven on by SS guards and Kapos (prisoners with authority over fellow inmates), constantly beaten and kicked, many were soon reduced to living wrecks. Some went mad. Most work was done manually. Even the rocks broken loose by blasting were removed by hand. Mining accidents were frequent.

In 12-hour shifts, the slave workers, overseen by civilian engineers, worked on many different jobs: pushing through Tunnel A and galleries beyond No. 42; levelling the circular galleries 25-42 with debris; pouring concrete; drilling ventilation shafts; removing the oil barrels and dismantling the giant oil tanks; laying train tracks; installing electric wiring, pipe systems, transformer stations, water pumps, and machinery; camouflaging the tunnel entrances and creating phoney rail complexes for deception at both mountain sides; building office huts at the site, and billet huts at Ilfeld and Harzungen (40 huts in all); and a thousand other jobs.

In addition, the slave labourers built their own concentration camp.

After the war, the camp was virtually razed to the ground, stone buildings being demolished and wooden huts being removed. In GDR times, only the central part of the camp – the open space from the Appellplatz to the coal shed (Block 19) – was made into a memorial site, the rest being made inaccessible to visitors. Of the foundations that were thus left to be seen, the largest was that of the U-shaped camp kitchen (Block 10). (Karel Margry)

Meanwhile, hidden under the trees and gradually disappearing under the undergrowth, remained the foundations of all the other buildings. However, all this changed with the demise of the GDR in 1990. Since then, the Memorial staff, with the help of youth volunteer camps, have systematically excavated and laid bare the remains of more huts and buildings. This is the camp laundry (Block 41). (Karel Margry)

Also open to inspection in GDR times was one of the two water reservoirs. (Karel Margry)

Located less than a kilometre from the southern exit of Tunnel B on the sloping edge of a valley, in its final form it comprised 56 living huts, three administrative huts, 12 economic huts, two bath houses, a hospital area of ten huts, a crematorium and a prison block ('the bunker'); improvements in the summer of 1944 included a water cistern, canteen, cinema, sports ground, and even for a while a prisoners' bordello, the latter frequented mainly by Kapos and foremen. The entire compound was surrounded by an electrified wire fence and 18 guard towers. The SS compound of 25 buildings

The delousing station (Block 32). During a delousing action, prisoners had to hand in their clothes and wait outside naked, in all weathers, while these were being disinfected. If that was not bad enough, their garments would be returned still wet from the cleaning, making the risk of catching a cold or pneumonia even greater. Delousing was ineffective anyway, because inmates from disinfected huts worked together with occupants of huts which had not yet been treated. (Karel Margry)

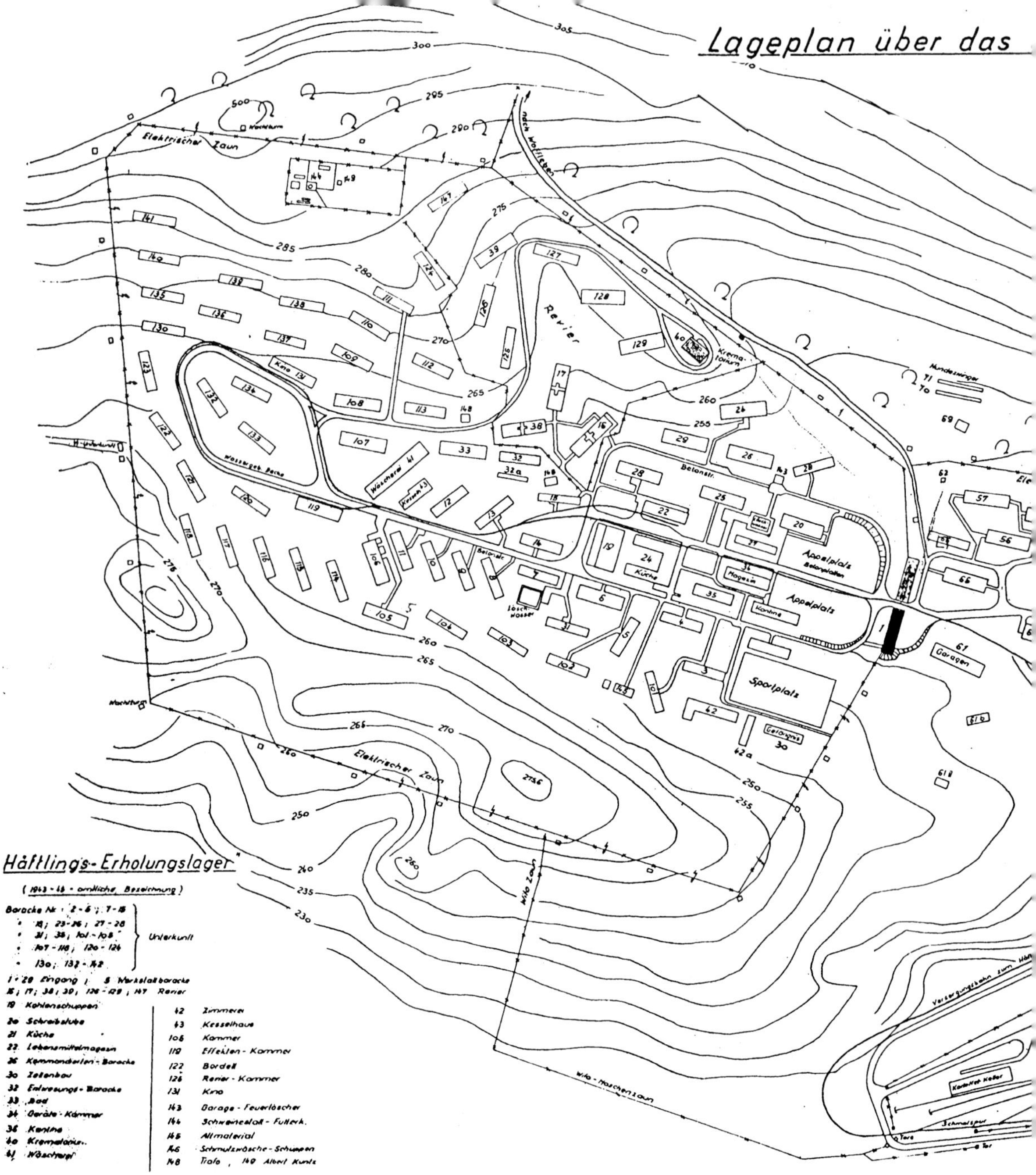

PRISONERS' CAMP

Living huts	Blocks 2-4, 7-15, 18, 23-25, 27-28, 31, 35, 101-105, 107-118, 120-124, 130, 132-142	Coal shed	Block 19	Carpenter's workshop	Block 42
		Kitchen	Block 21	Metal workshop	Block 42a
		Tool shed	Block 22	Boiler-house	Block 43
		Bordello	Block 26	Clothes storage	Block 106
		Prison	Block 30	Storage	Block 119
Hospital	Blocks 16-17, 38-39, 125-129, 147	Delousing station	Block 32	Cinema	Block 131
		Baths	Block 33	Fire-brigade	Block 143
Camp administration	Block 1	Storehouse	Block 34	Pigsty/Fodder store	Block 144
Gestapo office	Block 29	Canteen	Block 36	Re-usable materials	Block 145
Statistics office	Block 20	Crematorium	Block 40	Dirty laundry shed	Block 146
Workshops	Block 5	Laundry	Block 41	Transformer-station	Block 148

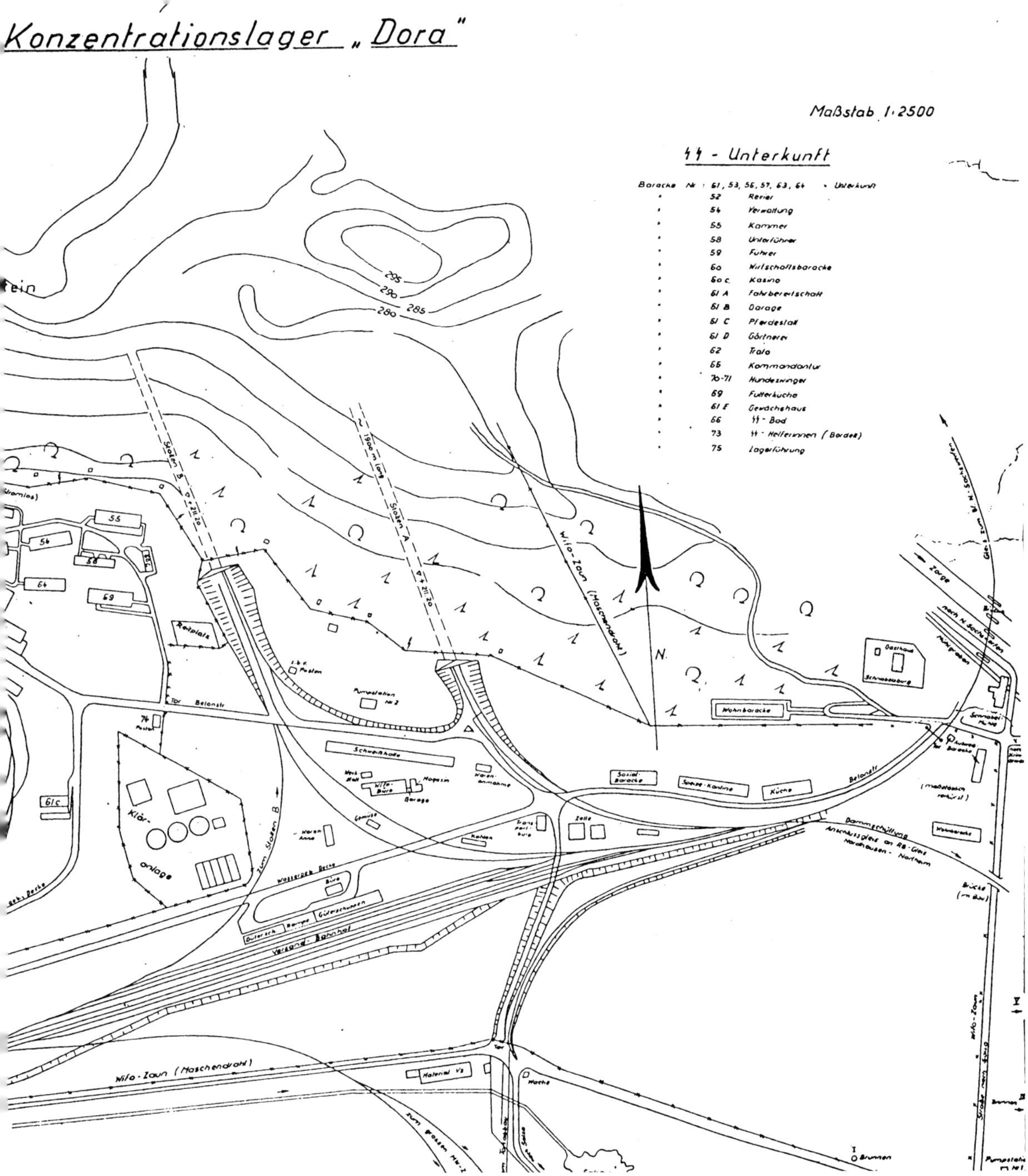

SS CAMP

Kommandantur	Block 65
Camp command	Block 75
Administration	Block 54
Officers' quarters	Block 59
NCOs' quarters	Block 58
Other ranks' quarters	Blocks 51, 53, 56-57, 63-64
Sick-bay	Block 52
Clothes storage	Block 55
Storehouse	Block 60a-60b
Mess	Block 60c
Drivers	Block 61a
Garages	Block 61b
Stables	Block 61c
Gardener	Block 61d
Greenhouse	Block 61e
Transformer-station	Block 62
Baths	Block 66
Kitchen	Block 69
Guard dogs	Blocks 70-71
Bordello	Block 73

Lay-out of the camp and the adjoining SS compound as it was in its final form in 1945 (Tunnels B and A are on the right).
(Gedenkstätte Mittelbau-Dora)

Block 119, the Effektenkammer (storage building). On arrival at 'Dora', prisoners had to hand in all their personal possessions which were then stored here. However, most inmates had been at Buchenwald before and already been robbed clean there, so the majority arrived with very little of their own. Prisoners assigned to the Effektenkammer-Kommando had therefore relatively little to do, and were thus considered lucky. (Karel Margry)

included a Kommandantur and administrative block, six barrack blocks for 900 guards, five living blocks for SS personnel, four economic blocks, a hospital, horse stable, garage, canteen, and a bordello.

The number of prisoners sent from Buchenwald rose rapidly: by the end of September there were 3,000, one month later 6,000, by the end of the

Block 125, one of the camp's ten hospital huts (and one of the few with a basement). Originally, Dora's Krankenrevier (sick-bay area) was small but, as the number of sick and injured inmates rose, it expanded, eventually encompassing a special section of ten huts, separated from the rest of the camp by a barbed-wire fence. Since the SS, for fear of contagious diseases, tended to avoid the hospital area, it was able to become a centre of the prisoners' resistance organisation. (Karel Margry)

year 10,000 – mostly Russians, Poles and Frenchmen, with smaller groups of Germans, Belgians, Italian military internees, Dutchmen and nearly three dozen other nationalities. By December 31, only 5,500 of these were living in the open-air hutted camp, the others were still in the deadly tunnels. Gradually, as the camp was enlarged, the others were transferred to it as well, finally regaining the light of day and fresh air. The last unfortunates did not come out until June 1944.

Owing to their bad accommodation, starvation, hard work and maltreatment, the death rate among the slave workers was appalling. Of some 17,500 inmates that had been sent to 'Dora' by April 1944, some 3,000 had perished. Their emaciated corpses were sent back to Buchenwald to be cremated. (This became unnecessary when 'Dora' opened its own crematorium on March 30, 1944.) Another 3,000 prisoners which had become too disabled or sick to be of any use were shipped off to other camps: 1,000 each to Majdanek on January 15 and February 8, and another 1,000 to Bergen-Belsen on April 8.

Meanwhile, the underground factory was rapidly taking shape. Tunnel A would soon reach its southern exit. Four more galleries, 43 to 46, had

Block 131, the camp cinema. Built in the summer of 1944, it had 200 seats. At a ticket price of 30 Pfennig, prisoners could watch selected movies and newsreels here. However, from January 1945, the building was used to house prisoners evacuated from other camps, up to 1,200 being crammed into it. (Karel Margry)

The camp's second water cistern.
(Karel Margry)

Today, there is again a wartime hut on the grounds of the 'Dora' Memorial. This particular specimen was found surviving in a former forced-labour camp in Nordhausen town. Rebuilt in 1991 on one of the valley terraces, on the site of the former Block 28, it is today used for exhibitions and as a seminar room.
(Karel Margry)

In this picture, taken in 1946 (when the camp housed German refugees), the same reservoir can be seen in the lower right corner. The huts in the foreground are Blocks 7 and 8, with 13 in the middle distance, and 32 (the delousing block) and 33 (the bathhouse) above that. Each prisoner's block divided into a sleeping compartment with a number of two-tiered bunks and an eating compartment with tables and stools. The huts were well supplied with heating appliances and sanitary facilities with running water.
(Gedenkstätte Mittelbau-Dora)

been shot through (Nos. 47 to 50 were never completed). In all, the slave labourers removed 125,000 cubic metres of stone, adding 12,600 square metres of floor to the existing 98,000. Every day, dozens of trains arrived bringing tons of building materials, tools and equipment. Starting on September 19, special trains carried the machines, equipment and personnel from the three V2 factory sites to Nordhausen.

On October 30, to ensure deliveries by the sub-contractors, Degenkolb created a special Führungsstab (Head Staff) under Hauptmann Dr Kühle, which had representatives with plenipotentiary powers at each of the major supplying firms. In December, this Führungsstab became even more important when it was given responsibility for the whole V2 contract.

On December 10, 1943, Speer, accompanied by Kammler and Degenkolb, came to Nordhausen for a personal inspection of the complex. He was impressed by the magnitude and speed of the whole project, but seems not to have been unduly moved by the misery of the slave workers, only worried lest they might lose too much of their effectiveness.

The camp prison (Block 30), also known as 'the Bunker'. A stone building in a remote corner of the camp (note the wall hiding it from view), it contained 32 cells of 2½ square metres each, in which sometimes up to 16 prisoners were confined at a time; an interrogation room, where prisoners were beaten up and tortured; and a cellar which the camp SS used as an air-raid shelter. The large building in the background is Block 42a, the metal-workshop. (GSDM)

The remains of the prison were laid bare in 1997 with the help of youth volunteers from various school educational projects. (Karel Margry)

In 2011, the remnants of the brick walls were topped by concrete additions for further protection and a concrete wall added to mark the former outer wall of the prison yard.
(Karel Margry)

During the time when 'Dora' was a GDR memorial, the only other intact building, apart from the crematorium, said to be original was this concrete structure located in the south-east corner of the camp. For years it was known as the 'Stehbunker' (standing bunker), purportedly a one-man prison cell used for isolation punishment. However, both claims were wrong. It was not an original building but a reconstruction, erected in 1974, of a building that had been there during the war; and it was not an isolation cell but a watchtower for the SS guards with an air-raid shelter below.
(Karel Margry)

The entire camp complex was surrounded by a double electrified fence guarded by watchtowers at regular intervals. Though difficult to match today because of the dense tree growth there, this is almost certainly the part closing off the valley at the western end.
(Gedenkstätte Mittelbau-Dora)

However, there is one other original building still standing, an unobtrusive small structure overlooked by most visitors. This is Block 145, the Altmateriallager (storage building for re-usable materials), down a path off the southern camp road.
(Karel Margry)

The camp crematorium. Initially, prisoners who had died at 'Dora' were sent back to Buchenwald to be cremated there but, as the number of dead grew, it was decided to build a crematorium on site. Erected up on the slope of the Kohnstein, under the trees and somewhat isolated from the rest of the camp, it was taken into use on March 30, 1944. A loop road through the sick-bay area led up to it (see the plan on pages 28-29).
(Gedenkstätte Mittelbau-Dora)

About the only building not pulled down after the war, the crematorium became the centre of the memorial site in GDR times, an exhibition being set up inside and many wreath-laying ceremonies taking place outside. However, with a new flight of steps having been laid out leading up to it, most visitors to the memorial were unaware that they were in fact entering the crematorium through the back doors. What is today the building's rear was originally its front.
(Karel Margry)

Another legacy of GDR times: the sculpture of five 'Dora' slave labourers by Jürgen von Woisky, dedicated in 1964.
(Karel Margry)

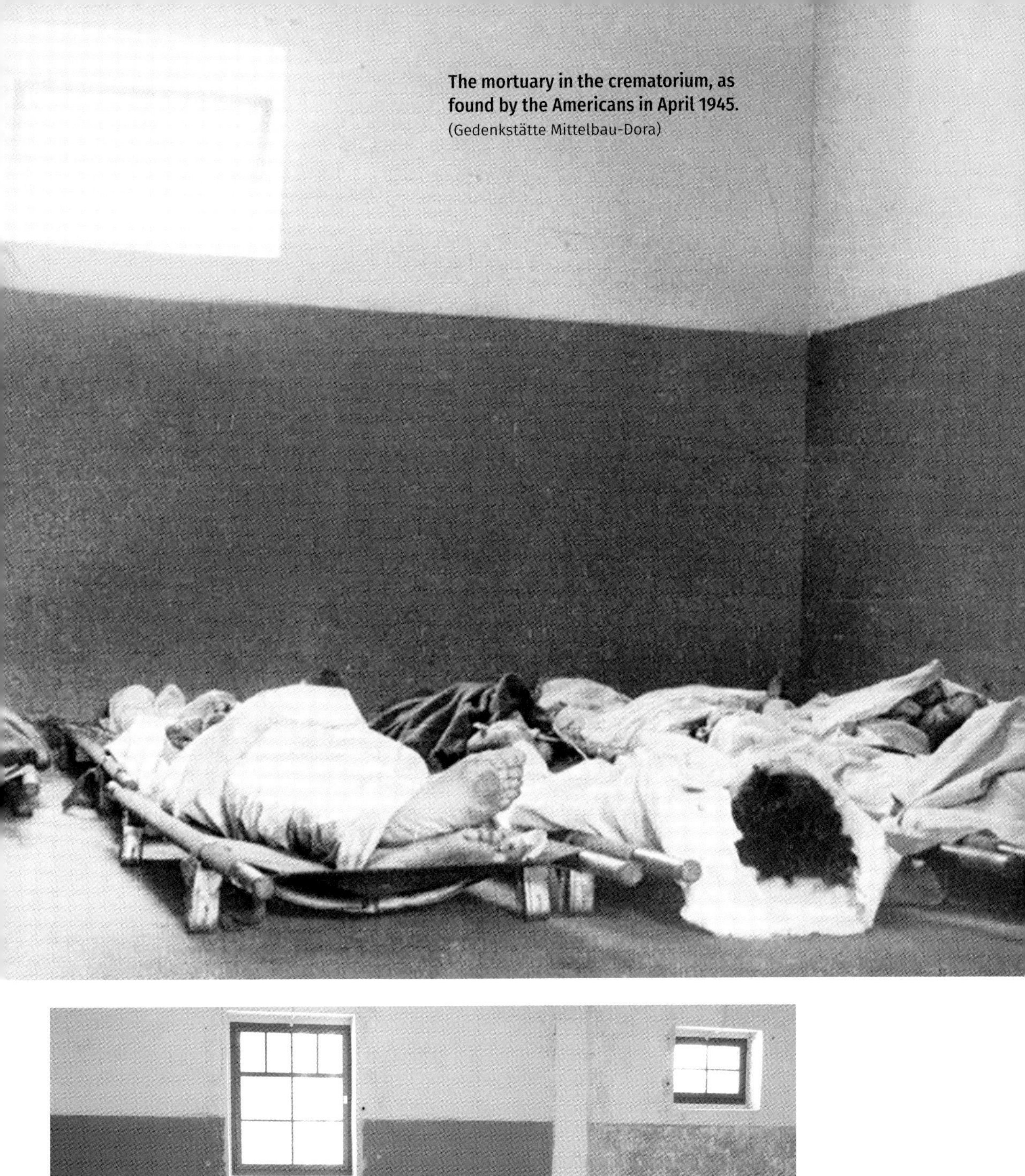

The mortuary in the crematorium, as found by the Americans in April 1945. (Gedenkstätte Mittelbau-Dora)

To create space for their exhibition, the East German authorities pulled down the dividing wall between the mortuary (on the left) and the adjoining room. (Karel Margry)

The crematorium had two ovens of a standard type produced by the Berlin-based firm of Kori GmbH and seen in other concentration camps too (e.g. Dachau, Neuengamme, Sachsenhausen, Ravensbrück, Flossenbürg, Gross-Rosen, Majdanek and Bergen-Belsen). This picture was taken on April 14, 1945, after the camp's liberation by American forces. A freed Polish inmate shows one of the ovens to Tech/5 John L. Lyndon of the US VII Corps. (USNA)

START OF V2 PRODUCTION

By now, the factory was ready to start tentative production. From early December, when the machines had been installed, all the prisoners, except for those building the camp outside, were employed at assembling rockets. The first three V2s rolled off the assembly line in Tunnel B on January 1, 1944. However, on arrival at Peenemünde, these three, Nos. 17001-17003, proved to have so many production faults that they could not be test-fired. When No. 17003 was finally launched on January 27, it failed and exploded. Further test launches at the new, SS-controlled, rocket test site 'Heidelager' near Blizna (in south-eastern Poland) were equally disappointing, most of them exploding in the air or at the start, and only 10 to 20 per cent hitting the target area.

The many failures were caused both by the immense technical complexity of the rocket missile itself (a V2 consisted of 20,000 different components)

Simultaneously with the construction of the slave labour camp, the underground tunnels were being converted into a production-line factory for V2s. The ladder-like plan of the complex was ideal for series production: goods trains would bring in raw materials via Tunnel A and supply the workshops in the side galleries, which in turn would supply components and sub-assemblies to the assembly line in Tunnel B, the V2 being built up as it passed along the galleries towards the southern exit. This is Tunnel B at the beginning of the V2 production line (which at the end of the war, when this picture was taken, began at Gallery 21, the stretch from 1 to 20 having been handed over to jet fighter engine production). Though Tunnel B had two standard-gauge railway tracks running through it, the special trolleys of the V2 assembly line ran on narrow-gauge tracks. In fact, the trolley line on the left is here partly covering one of the normal-width tracks. (BA)

Without proper captioning, identification of individual galleries within the Kohnstein mountain is not easy. Often, it is only from such clues as the type of V-weapon or components visible, the sort of machinery, the tunnel form, the height of the ceiling, the presence of railway tracks and other such details that one can determine which gallery one is in fact looking at. In this picture there are several clues. On the left is a jig for welding V2 fins; on the right lie a V2 turbo pump and a V2 hydrogen-peroxide ('T-Stoff') container, the latter complete with compressed-air bottles. Such components were made in Galleries 16-18 and 20-21. The circular ceiling indicates that it must be a gallery beyond No. 18 – so this could be either 20 (production of turbo pumps) or 21 (production of V2 parts). (BA)

and by the many possibilities for sabotage by the forced labourers. Measures to improve production quality were quickly taken. Countless directives and improvement proposals were sent from Peenemünde to Nordhausen (Von Braun himself visiting the factory on January 25). Simplifications found during production were introduced. Technically-trained prisoners were put in charge of and forced to oversee the work of fellow-inmates. Anti-sabotage measures were increased. Any negligence was now regarded as sabotage, and could lead to incarceration in the 'bunker' or death by hanging. One day (probably in March 1945), the guards hanged some 50 inmates in Gallery 41, tying a dozen at a time to a beam which was then pulled up by an electrical crane, and forcing the other prisoners to watch. To uncover resistance and sabotage groups, the Germans made extensive use of informers, both planted spies and prisoners betraying their fellow-inmates.

In the first month of production, January 1944, only 50 missiles were completed, i.e. less than two per day, but thereafter these figures rose steadily: 86 in February, 170 in March, 253 in April, 437 in May. Gradually,

One of the circular-type galleries as it looks today, pictured by American photographer Alvin Gilens. In 1994, Gilens extensively photographed the whole tunnel complex, the result of which was a photo exhibition and a photo book titled *Discovery and Despair. Dimensions of Dora*, published in 1995. The Niedersachswerfen gypsum factory, who own the Kohnstein mountain, are today no longer prepared to accept the legal risk of outside visitors entering unsecured parts of the tunnels, so we are very pleased that Mr Gilens has agreed to let us use his photos to illustrate the parts we could not visit. (Alvin Gilens)

the rocket was improved. For example, the introduction in May of glass-wool insulation between the rocket's fuel container and the sheet-steel outer skin (which would get very hot from friction during flight) lessened premature explosions by half. Reinforcing the missile's nose with an inner skin further reduced failures.

The V2s produced at Nordhausen were delivered without warheads and, initially, also without electrical systems. Well-camouflaged, the finished missiles were transported by train to the Demag vehicle works at Falkensee near Berlin, which installed the wiring, and from there to one of the Army Ammunition Establishments to receive the explosive warhead. From May, the installation of the electrical equipment was done in the Mittelwerk itself. For this, a special dust-free workshop had been built in the one of the underground galleries. Another special gallery was No. 41: its floor had been deepened by an extra 15 metres so that rockets could be set upright for final testing and checking. An especially-dangerous place in the assembly line was the galvanising shop in Gallery 39; prisoners assigned here were inexorably poisoned by the build-up of toxic fumes, the average life expectancy here being just one month.

At the start of the production line, in Galleries 23 or 24, were stored the big 6.15-metre-long half-sections of the V2 fuselage's middle part. In upright position, they almost touched the ceiling, and this probably explains why this picture has been captioned in some publications as showing 'concrete support pillars'! (BA)

This is either Gallery 25 or 26 – both were used to store the V2's mid-section fuel tanks, the ones in this picture being 'A-Stoff' (liquid-oxygen) containers. The V2's other main tank held a mixture of alcohol and water ('B-Stoff'). Delivered from elsewhere, these tanks were only given a pressure test before assembly into the V2. Note that this room has a second storey built in – a concrete floor standing on iron supports. This is a construction seen in many of the galleries. (BA)

Remains of a double storey survive in the underground darkness, this particular one being pictured in Gallery 45. (Karel Margry)

This is without doubt Gallery 29, the assembly line for the V2 combustion chamber. The view is from Tunnel A towards Tunnel B. Gallery 29 was one of those galleries which had been excavated deeper, to below ground-water level, so pumps had to be installed to keep them dry.

An incredible sight after half a century: V2 motors lying about in a flooded Gallery 29, pictured by Alvin Gilens in 1994.
(Alvin Gilens).

More V2 combustion units awaiting assembly into the rocket. The rail track shows that this is one of the main tunnels, probably off Gallery 29, and the absence of an assembly line suggests that it is Tunnel A rather than B. (BA)

Gallery 29 can today only be reached using a dinghy, but the long haul through complete darkness produces eerie comparisons indeed. (Alvin Gilens)

Metal-press workshops were in both Gallery 32 and 33. The huge Weingarten hydraulic press in the foreground was 6½ metres high. Both galleries are today flooded in several metres of water, but divers have confirmed that the presses' foundations are still there. (BA)

V2 tail units were assembled in Gallery 37. These are welding jigs for fitting the fins to the tail fuselage. With fins attached, the tail section stood nearly four metres (13 feet) high. The crooked roof beams are typical of the Wifo II galleries (Nos. 19-42).

Gallery 39 housed the 'Spritzerei', the dope-chamber where the V2 fuselage parts were galvanised and painted. This was one of most deadly galleries to work in, the toxic fumes from the varnish slowly poisoning those in the room. Workers assigned to this job would on average survive for a mere four weeks. Though the original caption to this picture described it as showing the dope-chamber, it cannot be the one in No. 39, since the configuration of that gallery is quite different and space there too confined for V2 tails to be set up like this. Probably this is an annexe to the main galvanising shop, perhaps in the adjoining Gallery 38. There is no means to check this, as No. 38 was completely blown up in 1945. (BA)

By the time the assembly line in Tunnel B reached this point, the rocket on the trolley was nearing completion. This picture, taken by the Americans after they captured the factory in April 1945, shows one that is complete except for its tail unit. Note the planking on the floor covering a stretch of the standard-gauge rail track. (IWM)

The same missile being inspected by members of a US Congressional Committee which visited 'Dora' camp and the underground factory on May 1, 1945, as part of their investigation into Nazi atrocities. Left to right are Representatives John M. Vorys (Republican of Ohio) and Ed V. Izac (Democrat of California); Senator C. Wayland Brooks (Republican of Illinois); and Lieutenant Colonel J. K. Reeson and Brigadier General John M. Weir of the US War Department. (USNA)

Just a few metres further on, on the outer assembly track, stood another V2. The chalking on it tells us that this particular missile was assembled by Combat Command R, 5th Armored Division, by order of Colonel Glen B. Anderson (the CCR commander). (Though captured by the 3rd Armored of US First Army, Nordhausen later came under control of the 5th Armored of Ninth Army.) Judging by the half-cut-away tail unit, it appears the CCR engineers intended this as a worked-out specimen to show the various internal parts of the rocket. (BA)

An abandoned V2 fuselage half, pictured by Alvin Gilens in 1994.

At the end of the assembly line, the V2 would reach Gallery 41, where, by means of a mobile crane, it would be put upright for final testing. No. 41 was the only tunnel sufficiently high to encompass for the 14-metre (47-feet) missile, its extra-deepened floor giving it a ceiling height of 15 metres. Note the pools of ground water.

In the underground world of the Kohnstein today, only the top of the test stand sticks out of the water. Too deep in the mountain for us to be allowed to photograph it, this spectacular picture was taken especially for us by Alvin Gilens in March 1998.

Beyond Gallery 42 began the section of the underground factory where, from August 1944 onwards, V1s were produced. This is most probably Gallery 43 (the upside-down chalking on the ceiling beam reads 'Stollen' [Gallery] and a half-hidden figure ending with '3'), and the sign at top left explains what was done here: 'Checking of construction and assembly (altitude steering unit)'. Note the different type of conveyor belt as compared to the V2. Gallery 43 was a deep-floor one and, instead of the more-common two storeys, it had three – this being the bottom floor. (USNA)

A different gallery, but still a nice comparison. This is Gallery 45. (Karel Margry)

PRODUCTION OF JET AIRCRAFT AND V1s MOVED INTO THE KOHNSTEIN

April-May 1944 marked the end of the first phase of the 'Mittelbau-Dora' complex, with several changes both in the camp, the underground factory and the company organisation.

With all prisoners now housed above-ground in 'Dora' and the camp facilities gradually being improved, life for the inmates had become a little more bearable – although of course the hard work and brutal treatment kept the toll in human lives high.

Also in April, the rapid growth of the Mittelwerk firm necessitated a revision of its internal organisation. Georg Rickhey, a Demag company director from the Ruhr area, was appointed General Managing Director, above all the other directors, and the various departments were differently organised. (The new position had earlier been offered to Degenkolb and to Figge, but both men had refused.) The reorganisation was not welcomed by all managers, and many judged Rickhey a failure and a loose-liver.

In the A4 Special Committee, there were changes too. About March, Director Degenkolb was relieved of his post and given a new task with the Reichsbahn. His old position was left vacant, Kunze and Figge taking over their chief's duties. In fact, the committee and its various sub-committees had achieved most of their tasks, and in due course most of them were reorganised or assigned to other jobs.

But perhaps the major change was that from April the Mittelwerk no longer had exclusive use of the underground factory or the Mittelbau area.

While the V2 scientists had successfully lobbied for priority and acquired the Nordhausen complex for its production lines, other German war industries, notably the aircraft industry, were also looking to get their factories underground. In early March 1944, faced with the increasing enemy attacks on aircraft factories and catastrophic bomber raids on German cities, Armaments Minister Speer and Generalfeldmarschall Erhard Milch, deputy chief of the Reich Air Ministry, jointly created the so-called Jägerstab (Fighter Staff) as a special agency to organise the upkeep of fighter production. Appointed executive chief of the Jägerstab was Karl Otto Saur, who soon not only streamlined fighter production but also successfully campaigned for more underground facilities for aircraft factories. At a Führer conference on March 5, Hitler decreed the transfer of the whole aircraft industry to bomb-proof factories.

Criticism, notably from Luftwaffe circles, that the Army's V2 programme was taking up inordinate amounts of manpower, resources and underground factory space (at the expense of, for example, fighter production and the Luftwaffe's V1 flying bomb project) seems not have been without effect on Hitler. At the March 5 conference, he had demanded a comparative inquiry to see whether the Mittelwerk resources and underground floor space could not better be allocated to aircraft

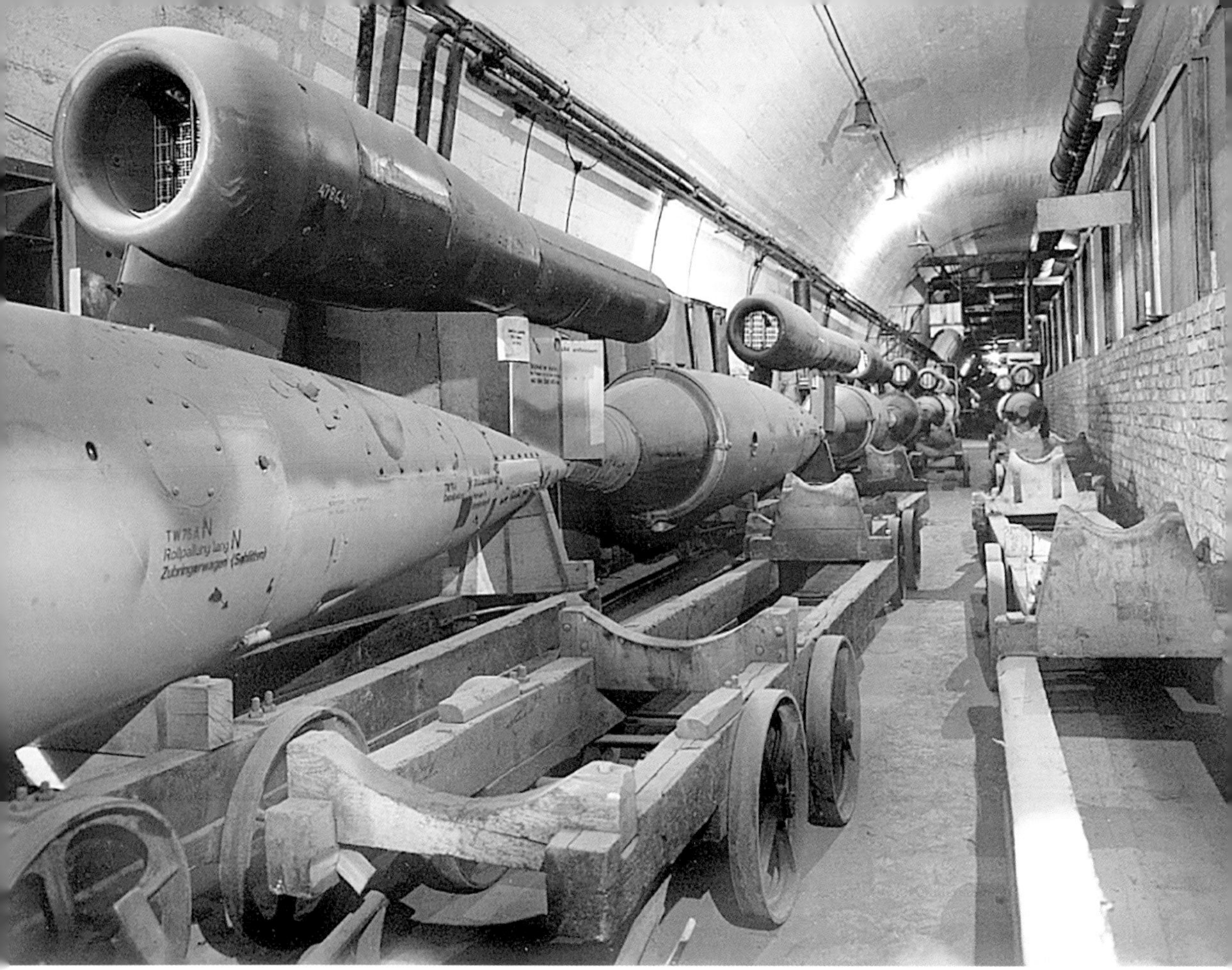

Completed V1s in main Tunnel A, south of Gallery 46. Tunnel A at this point had been divided in two by a brick wall, visible on the right. Note the specially-designed wooden trolleys for the V1. (IWM)

Ghosts from the past: the hull of a half-finished V1 in the nearby Gallery 45. As every participant in the guided tours provided by the Camp Memorial today will agree, to walk through the damp tunnels of the former underground factory among the rusted remains of Hitler's wonder weapons, the darkness pierced only by subtle lighting hung along the raised gangways, is a very strange and eerie experience. (Karel Margry)

Rusted V1 hulls piled up in a corner of Gallery 45. (Karel Margry)

Heaps of V1 parts lying about in Gallery 45. As a result of the 1948 Soviet demolitions, many of the double floors collapsed, causing the parts stored there to spill out on the bottom floor. (Karel Margry)

production. As a result, Hitler decreed that part of the Nordhausen underground factory was to be used for the production of jet fighter parts. In April, the Mittelwerk had to hand over the northern part of the complex, Galleries 1-20 (the former Wifo I), to the Junkers company, moving its own V2 factory to the remaining galleries 21-46. Transferring its aircraft engine factories at Magdeburg, Köthen and Leipzig, Junkers installed an assembly line for jet engines (code-name 'Nordwerk'). The work-force consisted of some 500 German specialists and 5,000 foreign workers. The latter, mostly Poles and Russians, were not concentration camp prisoners (they received wages, lived in requisitioned billets and did not wear the striped camp garments), and special measures were taken to ensure that they would not get in close contact with the 'Dora' inmates, though such contacts could not really be prevented when people had to work together.

Then, around the middle of June (no doubt influenced by the start of the V1 offensive against London on June 13), Hitler decided that V2 production be drastically reduced, to 150 pieces a month, and the manpower and resources

A heap of spherical holders for the V1 magnetic gyro compass. (Karel Margry)

thus freed be used to increase production of V1s and also jet fighters. Thus, the Army's rocket programme was trimmed in favour of two Luftwaffe programmes. As a consequence, V2 production fell from 437 in May to 132 in June and 86 in July.

Inevitably, the question arose whether production of V1s, until now concentrated at the Volkswagen factory at Fallersleben, should not also be

A V1 fuel tank.
(Karel Margry)

In April 1944, Galleries 1-20 were handed over to the Junkers company for the production of Jumo jet engines. Judging by the aircraft engine parts visible, this picture most likely shows one of their workshops. However, if we go by the chalk number visible on the machine on the right – A40 – this could equally well be Gallery 40, part of which was used from October 1944 for jet production too. (BA)

moved underground. The A4 Special Committee – now renamed the Sonder-Ausschuss z.b.V. (Special Committee for Special Purposes) – negotiated with the Volkswagen board and, in spite of strong opposition from VW director Anton Piëch, a decision was reached to transfer part of the V1 production to the Mittelwerk GmbH. Again, the V2 factory had to make room for a competitor, Galleries 43-46 being handed over to V1 manufacture in August 1944. From now on, the Mittelwerk housed the production of three different secret weapons: jet engines in Galleries 1-20 ('Nordwerk'), V2s in Galleries 21-42 ('Werk I'), and V1s in Galleries 43-46 ('Werk II').

The Junkers factory in the 'Nordwerk' produced two types of jet engines, the Jumo 004 B-1 and Jumo 004 B-4 for Me 262 and Ar 234 jet fighters respectively. In all, some 1,463 were delivered before war's end. In addition, in August, it received an order for 8,930 of the well-proven Jumo 213 engine. Production did not start until late 1944 and, by war's end, only some 800 had been completed.

The V2 factory in 'Werk I', though now reduced to 22 galleries, reached a steady production of about 600 missiles a month: 374 in August, 629 in September, 628 in October, 662 in November, 613 in December, 690 in January 1945, 617 in February and 362 in March. By the end of the war, a total of some 5,940 V2s had been made here.

The V1 factory in 'Werk II' was initially ordered to start production with

A toilet room, built into the side of Tunnel A. Sanitary facilities inside the mountain, especially in the first months, were extremely primitive, but were gradually improved later on. (Karel Margry)

400 pieces in September, rising to 1,000 the following month and to reach a steady production of 3,000 by December. Delivery had hardly begun when, in October, a new decree ordered the Mittelwerk to wind down V1 production until further notice, and only 238 were produced in November. However, the V1 soon regained its priority: in December production had risen again to 1,161, followed by 1,401 in January 1945, 2,275 in February, and 831 in March. In all, 'Werk II' produced over 7,500 V1s.

In October 1944, the Mittelwerk received orders to prepare a production line for the He 162 jet fighter, the so-called Volksjäger. This plane – cheap and simple, but very effective – was then still being developed by the Heinkel works (its first test flight was only on December 6), but time was now so short that series production was begun parallel with construction and testing. The Mittelwerk was both to manufacture the aircraft's body and BMW 003 engine and assemble complete aircraft (under the project code-name 'Schildkröte'). Since space was now extremely scarce, He 162 production had to be divided over various sites inside the mountain (Werk I's part of Tunnel

In one of the side rooms of Tunnel A, the Dora Memorial staff have set up a collection of interesting finds from the tunnels. With the stable air and temperature conditions inside the mountain, artefacts are best conserved by leaving them underground. (Karel Margry)

B; alcoves 17 to 27 in Tunnel A, and parts of Galleries 27, 31, 32, 37 and 40) and outside (notably the paper factory at Ilfeld). Only a few hundred He 162s were produced here before war's end.

OTHER UNDERGROUND FACTORIES IN THE 'MITTELBAU' AREA

Meanwhile, in addition to the V1 and jet factories now inserted in the Wifo tunnels, the construction of a large number of other underground factories was being undertaken in the immediate vicinity of the Mittelwerk. In March, Reichsmarschall Hermann Göring, chief of the Luftwaffe, had charged SS-Brigadeführer Hans Kammler – the same man who had so energetically provided the slave labour for the Mittelwerk – with carrying out the task of building the underground aircraft factories which Hitler had ordained. Since Kammler was an SS man, this of course gave his chief Himmler a perfect chance now also to gain power over the Reich's aircraft production (particularly the new jet fighters).

USE OF GALLERIES AND TUNNELS, APRIL 1945

'Nordwerk' (Jumo jet engine production)

1 Hospital
2 Jumo barrels and rods
3 Crankshafts, prop shafts
4 Machining miscellaneous parts
5 Storage miscellaneous parts
6 Machine-grindery
7-8 Jumo connecting rods
9 Jumo outer nose
10 Machining crankcases
11 Machining cylinder heads
12 Assembly Jumo engine
13 Machining Jumo parts
14 Storage V1 parts
15 Machining Jumo crankcases
16 Machining V2 turbo pumps
17 Machining V2 parts
18 Machining Jumo and V2 parts
19 Machining Jumo cylinder blocks
20 Machining V2 turbo pumps

'Werk I' (V2 production)

21 Machining V2 parts
22 Main stock and tool room
23 Sheet metal storage
24 Welding V2 centre section
25-26 Storage V2 tanks
27 Setting new machines
28 Assembly V2 nose
29 Assembly V2 power unit
30 Welding V2 centre section
31 Storage miscellaneous parts
32 Presses V2 parts
33 Presses V2 controls
34 Storage V2 metal
35 Storage V2 tails
36 Storage V2 parts
37 Assembly V2 tail
38 Storage V2 centre sections
39 V2 paint and galvanising shop
40 Machinery being set
41 Upright testing V2
42 Heating and vent machinery

'Werk II' (V1 production)

43-44 Machining V1 parts
45 Welding V1 skins
46 Welding and storage V1s
47 Sub-assembly V1 parts

Tunnel A

Galleries 1-26: Transport and supply railways
Galleries 27-41: V1 assembly line

Tunnel B

Galleries 1-20: Machining Jumo engines
Galleries 21-41: V2 assembly line

Oddly enough, there still exists some uncertainty today as to the exact number of side galleries completed inside the Kohnstein, the question being whether there were 46 or 47 (of the 50 planned). Almost none of the sketch plans published after the war agree on the number of galleries completed or the numbering system used. Part of the confusion is caused by the fact that chief engineer Albin Sawatzki, when planning the tunnels in 1943, out of some personal superstition did not want a gallery numbered 16; instead, the first gallery was given the number 0, the first 16 galleries thus becoming 0-15, and the next one after that 17. However, it is unknown whether this strange system was actually used inside the mountain. Solving the question today is thwarted by the fact that the whole northern end of the tunnel complex (from Gallery 4 backwards) has collapsed under the Soviet demolitions, making it impossible to count how many galleries are hidden under the debris there. At the other end of the tunnel, in the last two galleries but one, the original painted numbers '44' and '45' can still be seen on the wall, which would suggest a total of 46. However, the US Strategic Bombing Survey, who documented the complex before it was blown, produced a sketch which clearly shows 47 galleries. The simple solution that what the Americans called Nos. 1-47 was in fact the same as the German Nos. 0-46 does not hold out (even if the latter did include a No. 16), since the USSBS key to the use of galleries in many cases squares with what is known of the German one (e.g. they both have Gallery 29 as the room where V2 engines were assembled) whereas, if 1-47 was identical with 0-46, they should be one number different. The Dora Memorial hopes to once and for all solve the question when they carry out a new survey of the mountain, including a careful measurement of the collapsed parts, in the near future. The best plan available now is the one *(right)* which was prepared by the Bergsicherung (Mountain Security Authority) Ilfeld in 1991. It shows which Mittelwerk galleries have collapsed as a result of the Soviet demolitions (the dotted parts), and also how much of the mountain has been eaten away by the Niedersachswerfen quarry on the east side. (Note that this plan assumes the existence of a Gallery 0 and 16, and a total of 47 galleries.) The plan also indicates what is left of the adjoining B-11 and B-12 galleries. Now, with the tunnel system declared a protected site, the gypsum factory has to observe a 75-metre security distance at ground level and a 32-metre distance over the tunnels' ceiling. Though this will save the tunnel system, it means that continued quarrying will eventually (in a century or so) remove the whole of the Kohnstein's top and leave only a 'scalped' mountain. (Gedenkstätte Mittelbau-Dora)

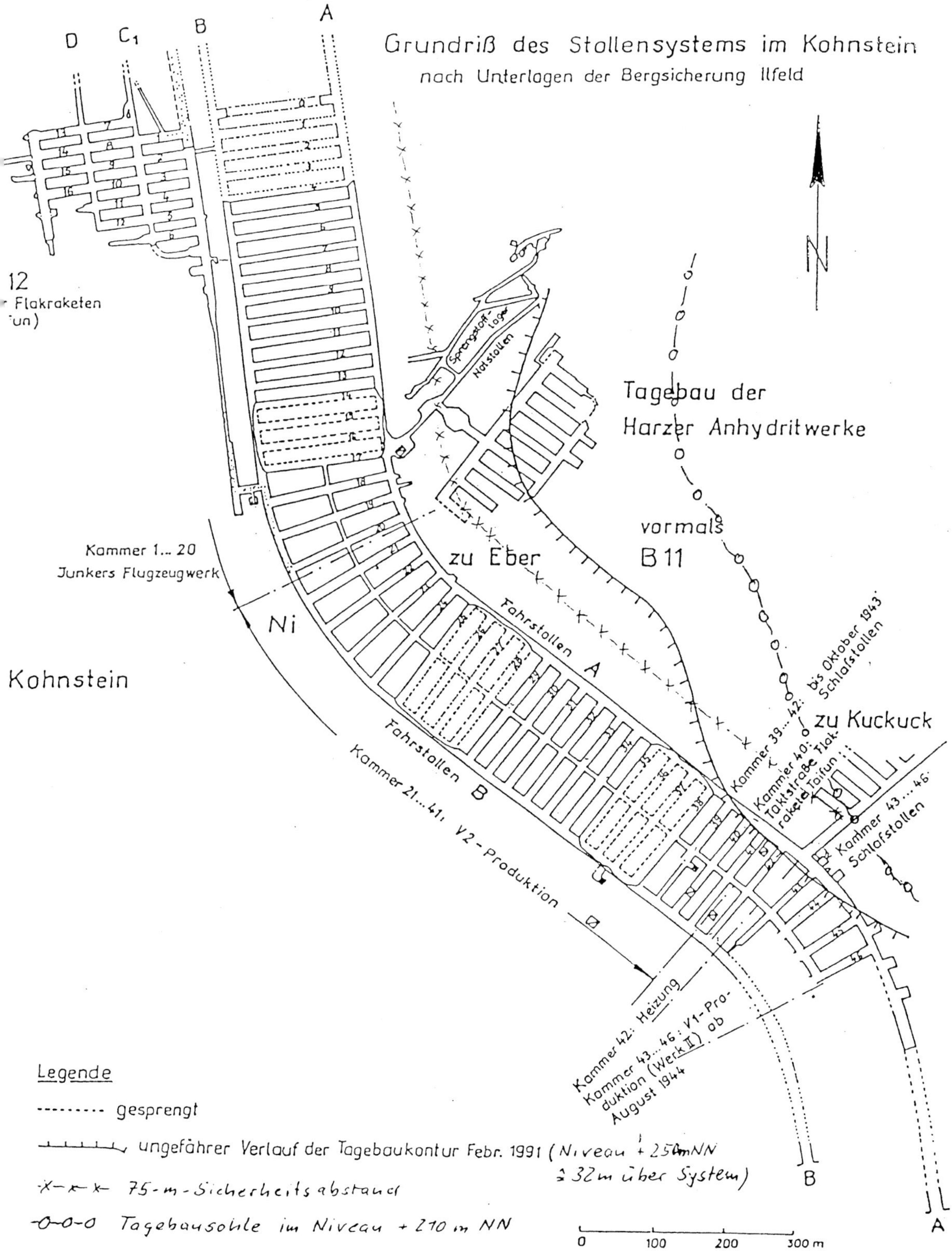

Grundriß des Stollensystems im Kohnstein
nach Unterlagen der Bergsicherung Ilfeld
D
C1
B
A
N
12
Flakraketen
Sprengstofflager
Notstollen
Tagebau der Harzer Anhydritwerke
vormals B 11
zu Eber
Kammer 1... 20 Junkers Flugzeugwerk
Ni
Kohnstein
Fahrstollen A
Fahrstollen B
Kammer 21...41, V2-Produktion
Kammer 39... 42: bis Oktober 1943 Schlafstollen
zu Kuckuck
Kammer 40: Taktstraße Flakrakete Taifun
Kammer 43... 46: Schlafstollen
Kammer 42: Heizung
Kammer 43...46: V1-Produktion (Werk II) ab August 1944
Legende
gesprengt
ungefährer Verlauf der Tagebaukontur Febr. 1991 (Niveau + 250 m NN ≙ 32 m über System)
75-m-Sicherheitsabstand
Tagebausohle im Niveau + 210 m NN
0
100
200
300 m

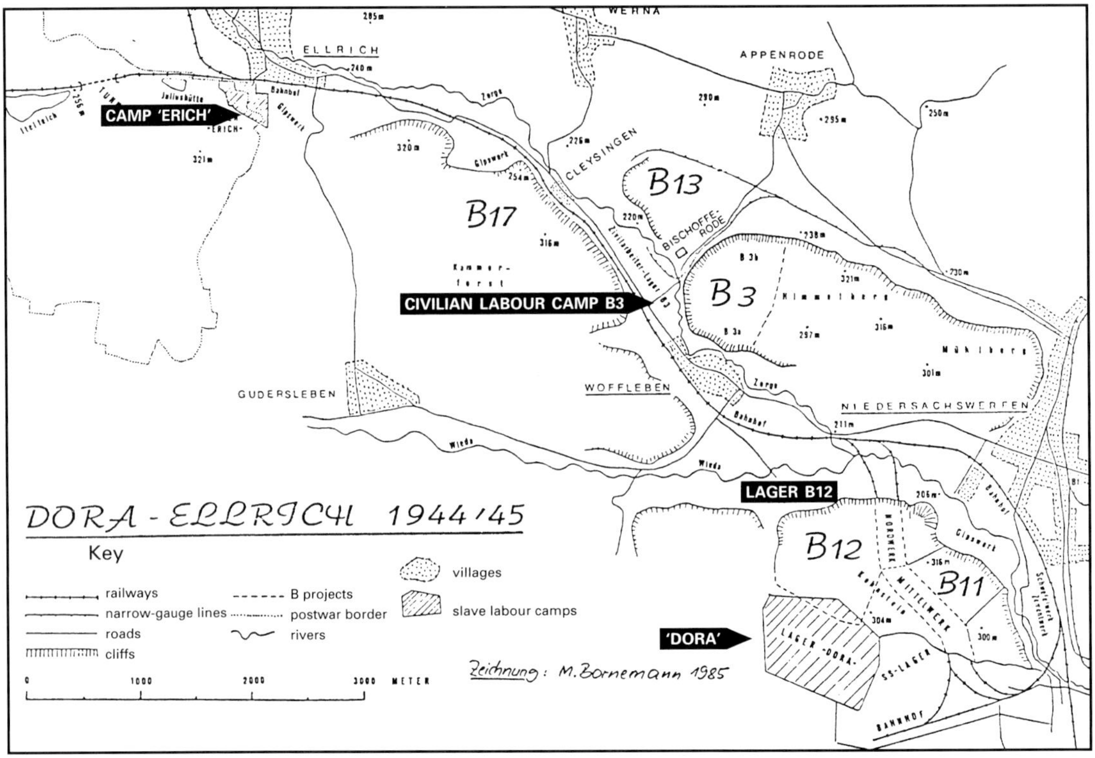

From May 1944, the Germans began the construction of several other secret underground aircraft factories near Nordhausen, not just in the Kohnstein, but also in the Himmelberg just to the north, and elsewhere. Directed by the SS-Sonderstab Kammler and using slave labourers, the building projects themselves were known by code-designations (B-3, B-11, B-12, etc). (Map by Manfred Bornemann)

For his new task, Kammler created a Sonderstab (Special Staff), made up of specialists from his own SS-Amtsgruppe C, the Wehrmacht and the Luftwaffe and divided into four Special Inspection Staffs, which drew up a list of construction projects to be carried out. These divided into A, B and S projects: 'A' projects were bomb-secure spaces to be built in already-existing underground complexes (caves, tunnels, mines, etc); 'B' projects were bomb-secure spaces to be newly built; and 'S' stood for 'Special' projects.

Projects in the Mittelbau area were planned and overseen by Special Inspection Staff II, led by SS-Hauptsturmführer Wilhelm Geissen, with headquarters at Halle. They included:

Project A-5: Twelve kilometres west of Nordhausen, in the natural caves at Uftrungen near Rottleberode (a protected site since 1922), the Junkers factory at Schönebeck in April 1944 installed a production line for Jumo 004 B-4 engines. In all, 8,000 square metres of cave floor were used. A railway line connected the site with the main line at Rottleberode.

Project B-4: Near A-5, in the gypsum massif south of the village of Stempeda, five separate galleries were planned to be dug into the mountain face, totalling 3,000 square metres. In the end, only three were started and, by war's end, only 592 square metres had been completed. The slave workers for both A-5 and B-4, some 900 on average, were housed in Lager 'Heinrich', a

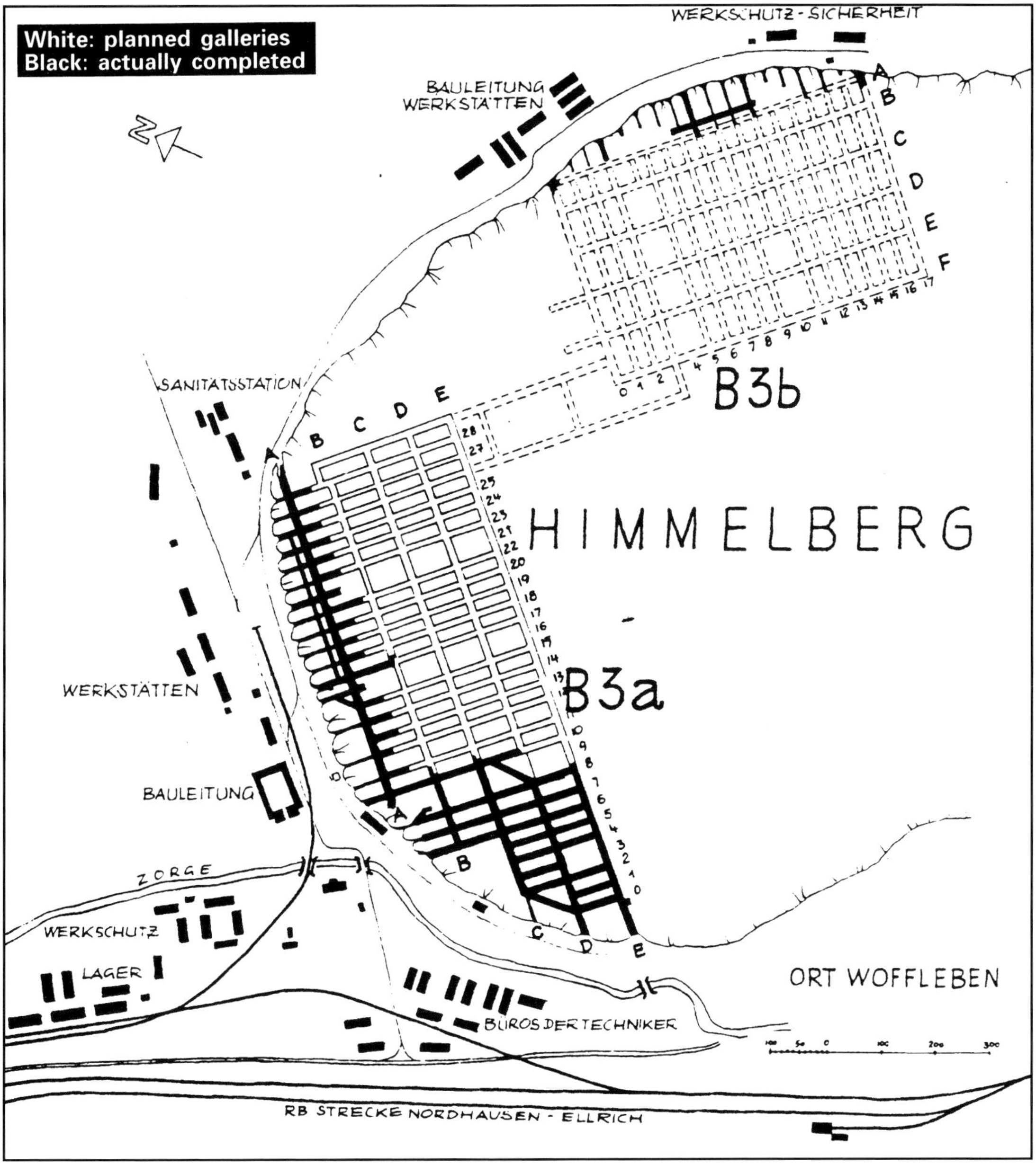

Projects B-3a and B-3b, in the Himmelberg north of Woffleben, were planned to eventually encompass 130,000 square metres of underground space. By war's end only about one-third of this (the parts drawn in black) had actually been completed and only B-3b taken into use. (Plan by Fred Dittmann)

requisitioned porcelain factory on the northern edge of Rottleberode.

Project B-3a: In the 60-metre-high cliff of the Himmelberg massif at Woffleben, just north of the Kohnstein, a large number of galleries were started, three in the southern face and over 20 in the western, the plan being to create a grid of a few long galleries connected by many lateral ones to a total of 130,000 square metres. Unusual here was the presence of soldiers from a Wehrmacht engineer company from Holzminden, who used the project to try out experimental drilling equipment. Only about one-third

Closed, like the Mittelwerk, by Soviet demolitions after the war, part of the B-3a tunnels was opened in the 1980s by the East German authorities to install a mushroom nursery. The entrance to it was made through Tunnel 10 on the west side of the Himmelberg. After the demise of the GDR, the underground farm passed from collective to private ownership. (Karel Margry)

(45,000 square metres) of the planned gallery space was actually completed, rocket missile production facilities (code-name 'Hydra') moving into the southern section in February 1945.

Project B-3b: Also in the Himmelberg, to the east of B-3a, near Appenrode, some ten galleries were started in the autumn of 1944, planned to be eventually linked to B3a by two galleries (total 100,000 square metres). In early 1945, the work here was abandoned in favour of another project, S-3 near Ohrdruf in Thuringia. The whole B-3 complex (code-name 'Anhydrit') was serviced by a system of narrow-gauge and normal railway tracks and linked to the main Reichsbahn system. Workshops, offices, transformer stations, pump-rooms, and billets for civilian personnel were in a hutted camp built between Woffleben and Bischofferode.

Slave labourers for both B-3a and B-3b were in hutted camps at Ellrich (camp 'Erich', around 8,000 inmates), Harzungen (camp 'Hans', 4,000 inmates) and Bischofferode (camp 'Anna', 500 inmates), all sub-camps of Buchenwald, later of 'Dora'. The life of the prisoners here – mostly Russians, Poles, Hungarian Jews, gypsies, Frenchmen and Belgians – was made even more miserable because the camps were up to 15 kilometres distant from the work sites, and they had walk there every morning and back in the evening, or travel in overfilled, open trains in all weathers.

Project B-11: In the Kohnstein, between the northern exits of the Mittelwerk complex and the gypsum quarry at Niedersachswerfen, a huge new tunnel complex (code-name 'Zinnstein') was started in May 1944, planned to produce 80,000 square metres of underground factory space. By

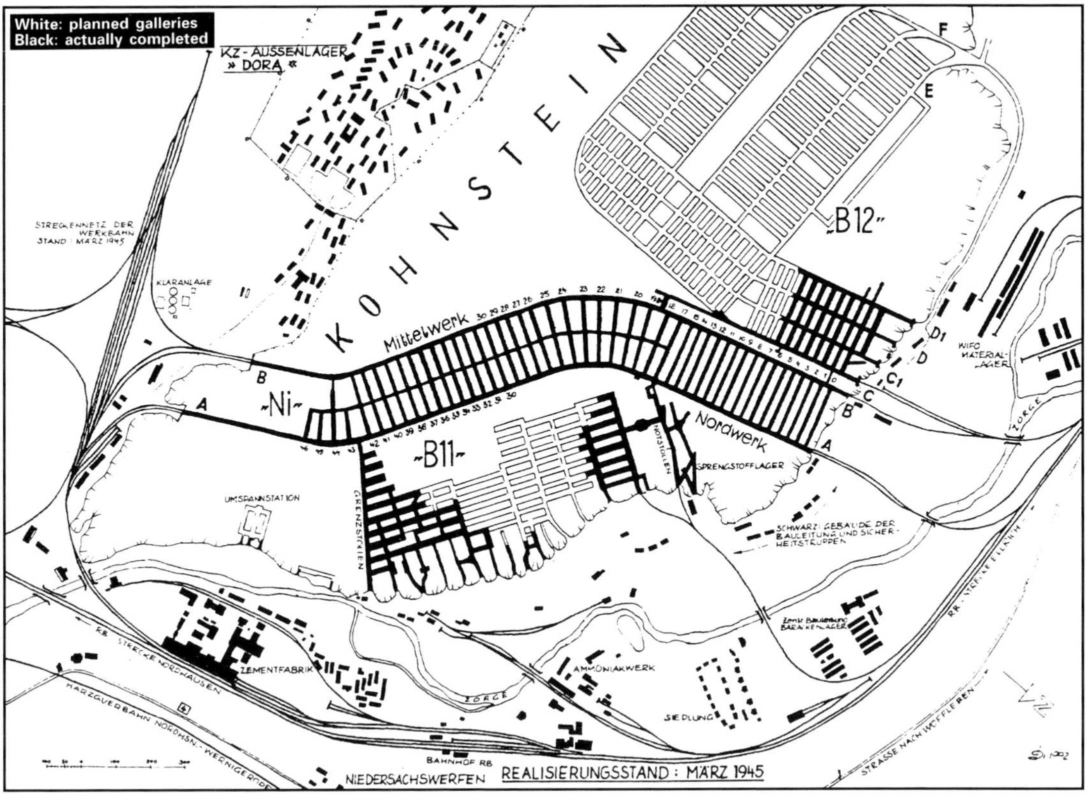

Even larger were the two projects planned on either side of the Mittelwerk complex in the Kohnstein, B-11 and B-12. Again, only a small part of the underground space planned was ever completed (about 65 per cent of B-11 and only five per cent of B-12), and about half of that actually taken into use by the aircraft industry before war's end.
(Plan by Fred Dittmann)

September, a force of 2,000 civilians and 2,500 slave labourers (from 'Dora' and from the B-3 camps at Ellrich and Harzungen) were at work here. In the autumn, sub-contractors of the Mittelwerk GmbH installed a hydrating factory producing aircraft fuel here (code-name 'Kuckuck I'), using 30,000 of the 53,000 square metres of finished galleries. Also planned here, but partly outside the mountain, was a liquid oxygen factory ('Eber'), liquid oxygen being one of the two propellants for V2s. However, of the planned 15 aggregates and six reservoir containers, only six of the former and two of the latter had been installed by war's end, and no liquid oxygen was ever produced here.

Project B-12: Also in the Kohnstein, on its north side and immediately adjacent to the Mittelwerk tunnel complex, was to come a gigantic underground aircraft factory of over 600,000 square metres – larger than both the Mittelwerk and B-11 taken together – a project that would take years to complete (code-name 'Kaolin'). This was one of two giant sheltered aircraft factories ordered by Hitler on April 6, 1944, this one to house production lines of the Junkers company (the other factory was to be in a giant bunker). By the time work was halted in April 1945, the four main galleries – C, D, E and F – had only advanced some 300 metres into the mountain, and eight to ten lateral galleries had been completed, totalling some 30,000 square

B-11 has now almost completely disappeared by decades of post-war quarrying. This is the view of the Kohnstein and the site of B-11 as seen from the Mühlberg. Niedersachswerfen and the gypsum factory are on the far left. (Karel Margry)

metres. Some 15,000 of these had been taken into use for production and assembly of He 162 jets. Slave labourers for B-12 came from the B-3 camp at Ellrich, and from a smaller B-12 camp (1,600 inmates) set up at Woffleben in January 1945.

Project B-13: This was not an underground installation, but an umbrella term for the construction of the infrastructure (roads, railways, bridges, etc) for B-3, B-11, B-12 and B-17. A major project was the construction of a new Reichsbahn line through the Helme river valley between Nordhausen and Osterhagen to unburden the existing line from Nordhausen via Ellrich to Northeim further north through the Zorge valley, now so heavily used for the war industry concentrating in this part of the Harz. The work was done by slave labourers organised

The B-12 tunnels were reopened by the GDR authorities in 1965-66 and converted into a cold-storage warehouse for fruit, vegetables and tinned products for the surrounding region. This is the entrance to Tunnel C, opened in May 1965. (Karel Margry)

A deserted loading ramp hides the entrance to Tunnel D today. (Karel Margry)

in so-called SS-Bau-Brigaden (SS Construction Brigades), transferred here from cities in the Ruhr area and each composed of between 500 to 1,800 men. Bau-Brigaden 3 and 4 arrived in May 1944, Bau-Brigade 5 in August-September, and Eisenbahn-Bau-Brigade 2 in September. Brigade 5 was later split to form Bau-Brigade 1 and Eisenbahn-Bau-Brigaden 1 and 3. Several small camps for them were built: for BB3 at Wieda, Osterhagen, Mackenrode and Nüxei (300 inmates each); for BB4 at Ellrich (some 950 inmates) and Günzerode (150); for BB1 at Sollstedt (450), for EBB1 at Neusollstedt (550), for EBB2 probably at Heringen (500) and for EBB3 at Kelbra (number of inmates unknown).

Project B-15: Apart from that it was located near Ellrich, little else is known of this project.

Project B-17: In a closed-down quarry in the Kammerforst forest near Ellrich, two galleries totalling 2,000 square metres were dug to accommodate a filling station (code-name 'Kuckuck II') for the aircraft fuel factory in B-11.

With more and more factories from all over the Reich transferring to central Germany, and concentrating in the Mittelbau region, this part of the Harz was rapidly becoming the industrial centre of the Reich, with the underground facilities of the Kohnstein as its heart. By war's end, the Mittelwerk company employed some 8,000 civilian workers and 25,000 slave labourers in the Nordhausen area.

With ever more slave labourers being sent to the Mittelbau region, and with new smaller camps springing up all over the area, the three main camps – 'Dora', Ellrich and Harzungen – were designated Mittelbau I (Dora), Mittelbau II (Ellrich) and Mittelbau III (Harzungen) on September 10, 1944.

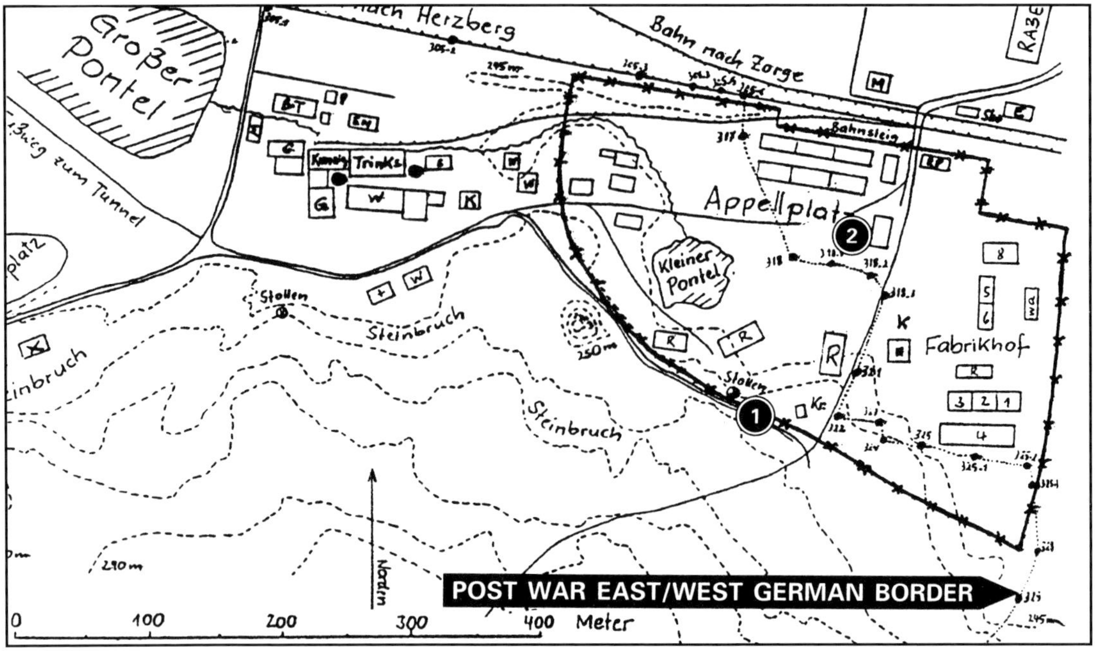

The slave workers for B-3, B-11 and B-12 were housed in camp 'Erich' at the village of Ellrich, five kilometres further west along the Zorge valley from Woffleben. Conditions in this sub-camp were at times more deadly than at 'Dora'. Key to buildings: [K] Kitchen, [X] Quarantine, [P] Stables, [R] Sick bay, [Kr] Crematorium, [RP] Guardhouse. The SS were billeted in the houses and factories around the camp. (Map by Manfred Bornemann)

All were still Aussenlager (sub-camps) of Buchenwald. However, to reflect the growing importance of 'Dora', its status was changed. On October 1, 1944, it was made a Hauptlager (Main Camp), independent of Buchenwald, the camps in the region becoming its Aussenlager. On the day the new set-up came into effect, October 28, the number of inmates (all camps together) was 32,532.

THE SS TAKES FULL CONTROL

Meanwhile, Himmler had successfully continued his campaign to gain complete power over all of the Third Reich's secret weapons. In the aftermath of the July 20 attempt on Hitler, he had seized direction of the Army's armaments department and thus gained total control of Peenemünde and the rocket programme. In August, he appointed Kammler (promoted to SS-Gruppenführer) his Plenipotentiary for the A4 Programme. In November, Hitler put Kammler in charge of various development projects for anti-aircraft rockets. But Himmler also wanted his SS to control the V1 and jet fighter programme. The first was achieved on January 31, 1945, when Kammler became commanding general of the Armeekorps z.b.V, responsible for deployment of all V-weapons; and the second in late February, when Kammler was in addition to all his other functions appointed General Plenipotentiary of the Führer for Jet Fighters.

In late January 1945, Kammler ordered a final concentration of all

After the war, Ellrich became an East German border town, off-limits to everyone except local inhabitants and GDR border police. In fact, 'Erich' is probably unique in being the only former Nazi concentration camp cut through by the Iron Curtain – the East German border security strip running right through the site where it had been. However, the high ground immediately overlooking it was West-German and, with access to the camp itself being impossible, a memorial stone ([1] on the plan) was set up here. (Karel Margry)

With the German reunification, the site finally became freely accessible again, and in May 1994 the Louvain branch of the Belgian camp survivors association erected a new memorial, this time on the actual spot ([2] on the plan). In 1998, a youth summer-camp unearthed the foundations of a camp hut and a watchtower and more remains have been laid bare since. Today, the site is an official memorial, several information panels having been set up in 2010. (Karel Margry)

scientific, experimental and production capabilities in the Mittelbau area: a new Entwicklungs-Gemeinschaft (Development Association), headed by the scientist Alfred Buch, was to unite all firms and institutes involved in flak missile research, all of which were required to move to the Mittelbau area. Responsible for directing development and testing would be a new agency created by the Armaments Ministry, the Arbeitsstab (Work Staff) Dornberger, while production would be coordinated by the old Special Committee.

In early February, the Arbeitsstab Dornberger set up headquarters at Bad Sachsa, 20 kilometres north-west of Nordhausen. One by one, the development firms involved – the Electromechanische Werke GmbH (the old Heeresversuchsanstalt Peenemünde, now changed to a private firm), Ruhrstahl AG, Gyroskope AG, Walterwerke AG, the Henschel and Dornier aircraft works, etc – moved their establishments to the Nordhausen area.

Personnel and equipment from Peenemünde – moving by train, car, truck

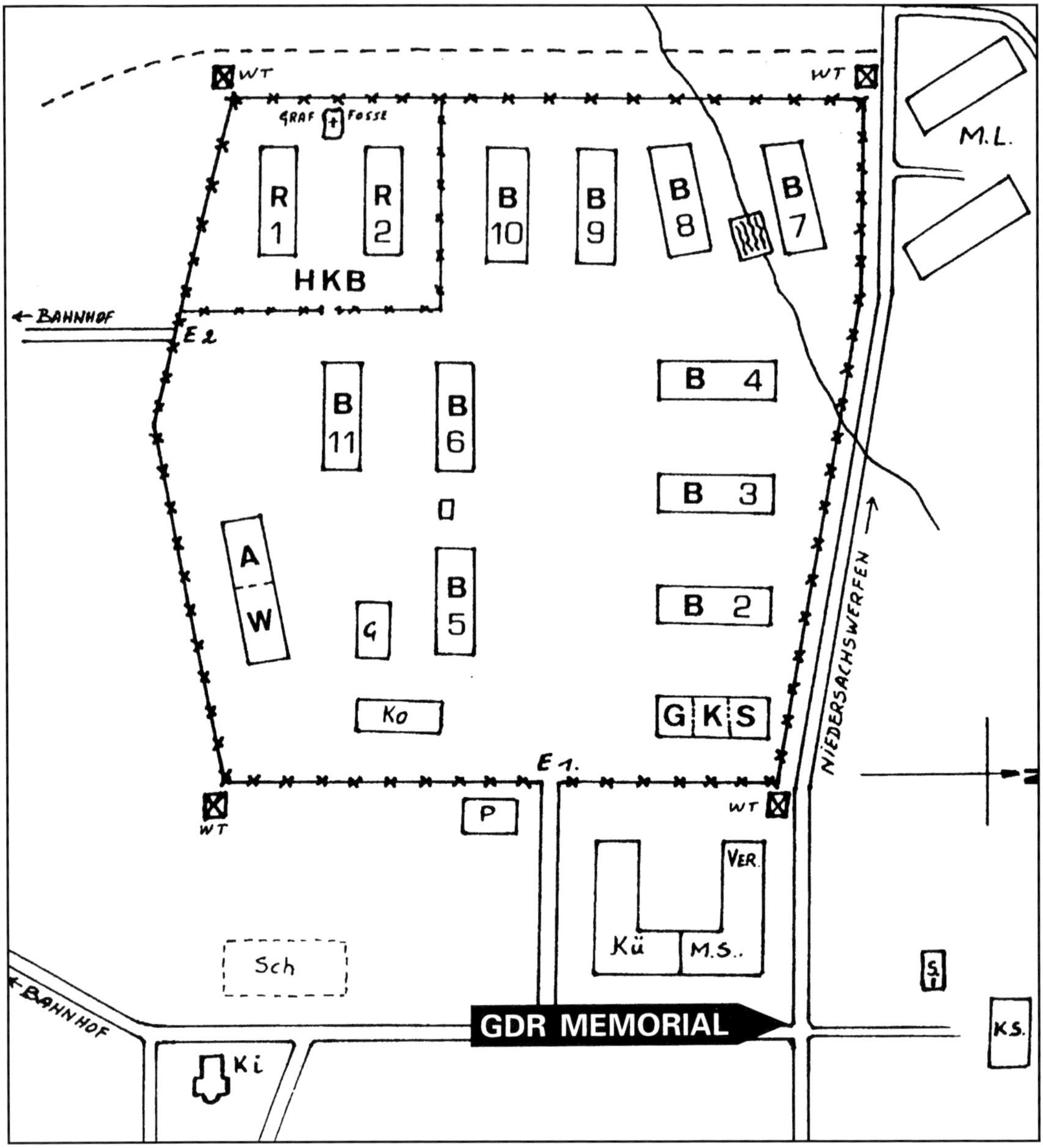

Slave workers for B-3 and B-11 were also at Harzungen, located three kilometres east of Niedersachswerfen. [R] Sick bay, [GKS] Storage rooms, [Kü] Kitchen, [AW] Baths/WC, [P] Guardhouse. (Maurice Bouchez)

and river barge – settled down in Bleicherode, 15 kilometres south-west of Nordhausen. (Travelling there by car in early March, von Braun was put out of action when he broke his arm in a car accident.) The research workshops and laboratories were provisionally set up in the nearby salt mines at Bleicherode, Neubleicherode and Sollstedt but, with the war obviously coming to its end, no serious work was ever done there.

Also in February, the Mittelwerk was ordered to take up series production of yet two more secret weapons, both small anti-aircraft rocket missiles and seen as the last-ditch weapons against the enemy air onslaught: the Taifun

(a slim 1.9-metre-long ground-to-air missile weighing 19 kilos) and the Orkan (an 81-centimetre-long air-to-air missile weighing four kilos). Of 70,000 Taifuns ordered, 50,000 were to be of the 'P' (solid fuel) and 20,000 of the 'F' (liquid fuel) type. In March, Taifun production facilities at Oppau, Piesteritz, Linz, Trostberg, Rotterdam, Haarlem and other places were transferred to the Mittelwerk. A production line was set up in the finished galleries of complex B-3a at Woffleben, but production never really got off the ground. When the war ended, only some 800 Taifuns, mainly of the P type, had been made here. As for the Orkan, it appears some 6,000 were manufactured, also in B-3a.

Earlier, in December 1944, the Henschel firm had already transferred part of its Berlin-Schönefeld factory to B-3a, their leading rocket scientist Professor Herbert Wagner installing research and production workshops

A memorial from GDR times on the corner of Am Hegeberg and Dorfstrasse marks the site. (Karel Margry)

An original camp hut survives on the spot. (Karel Margry)

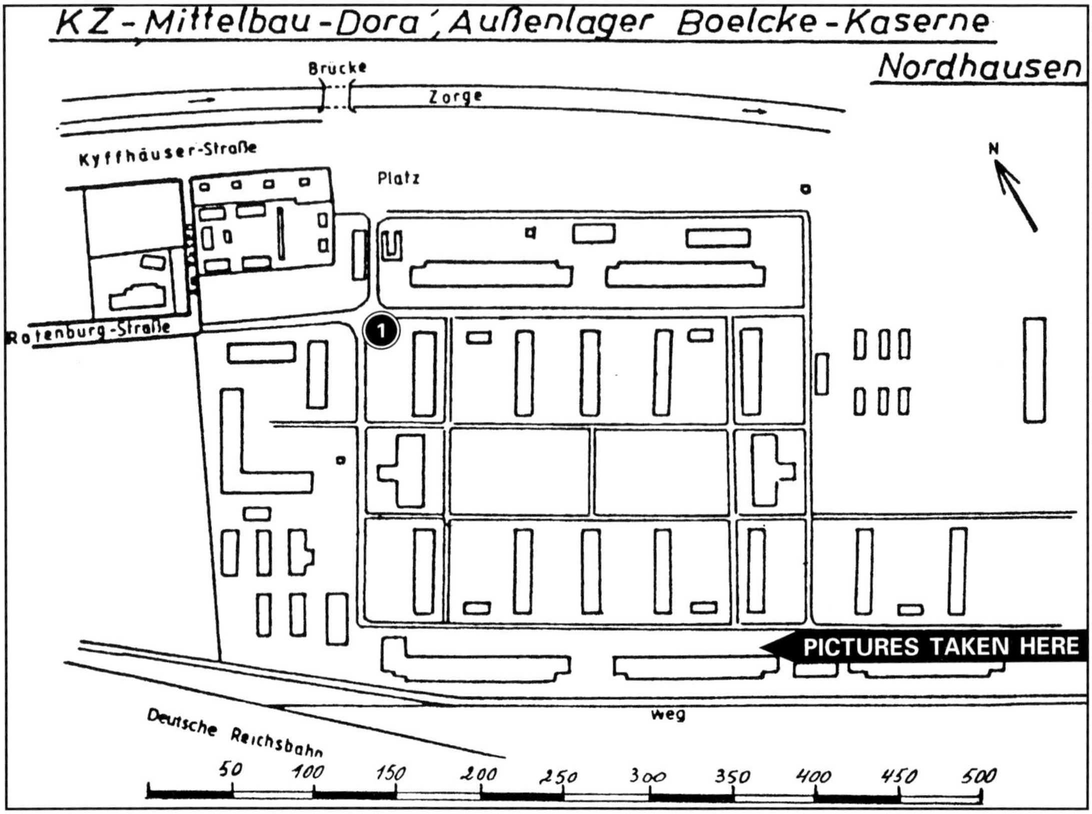

In January 1945, the SS took over the Boelcke-Kaserne, a Luftwaffe barracks on the other side of Nordhausen town (see map on page 10), to cope with the rising number of sick and invalid inmates. In the weeks following, prisoner groups arriving from other camps were also diverted there, and by early April some 3,500 inmates – French, Belgians, Poles, Russians, Germans – were accommodated here.

there for Hs 117, Hs 298 and Ruhrstal X4 air-to-air missiles and for Ruhrstahl X7 anti-tank and ground-to-air guided missiles. The Hs 117 even reached series production (some 1,400 were made), but a Kammler order on February 6 forbade further production of all four types, although research on the Hs 117 and X4 could continue.

Finally, and completely unannounced, on March 5, the main staff of the Armaments Ministry moved into the Mittelwerk. Its chief, Karl Otto Saur (Speer's deputy since July 1944), had first ordered its evacuation from Berlin to Blankenburg in the Harz in February. When rumours sprang up that Blankenburg would be bombed, Saur, overriding all protests, demanded refuge in the underground shelter. One half of the offices in Gallery 1 were to be made available; they were luxuriously fitted out with glass doors, carpets and heated baths. To the prisoners of 'Dora' who saw them, these rooms and their occupants seemed like from another world. (Saur's staff also took over galleries in the nearby Mühlberg, hitherto used by the people of Niedersachswerfen as air raid shelter.)

Between all the new staffs, industries and institutes moving in with their personnel and machines, occurred the far more dramatic arrival of thousands of slave prisoners who had been evacuated from other camps.

These wretched creatures arrived sick and hungry, having travelled for days in open trains in freezing cold, often without food or water. Many had died on the way. The first group, 1,000 prisoners from Buchenwald, arrived on January 24. It was followed in the next weeks by three from Auschwitz (some 4,000 persons in all), two from Gross-Rosen (4,700), one from Ravensbrück (992), again two from Gross-Rosen (5,324), and, in March, by one each from Bunzlau (441) and Aslau (487). Most of these 17,000 new inmates came to 'Dora', which was completely flooded by the new influx. The camp cinema (Block 131) was vacated and 1,200 crammed into it. On January 10, 'Dora' opened a sub-camp in a Luftwaffe barracks in Nordhausen, the Boelcke-Kaserne, which it used to accommodate sick prisoners, and the whole of the Gross-Rosen transport of February 16 (3,501 persons) was diverted there, as were the 487 inmates from Aslau on March 19.

Some of the new arrivals were put to work, but the majority was far too weak or sick to do any labour. The camp crematorium could not cope with all the dead and, in late February, corpses had to be burned in pyres in open air. On March 8, another transport of 2,250 sick and invalid inmates was shipped off to Bergen-Belsen.

With the inmates from evacuated camps came the SS guards and officers of these camps, many of them even more cruel and brutalised than those at 'Dora'. The reign of terror worsened. The number of dead from beatings and executions rose. An attempt by Russian and Polish inmates to break out of the 'bunker' on March 9 ended in them being massacred by the SS. There followed several mass executions on the roll-call square, some 52 inmates being hanged on March 10 and another 57 on March 20-21.

FINAL DAYS

With enemy armies closing in from east and west, preparations were made to defend the Kohnstein. A Wehrmacht battalion was stationed at Ilfeld and several Volkssturm (home guard) companies organised. However, the inevitable end could no longer be averted. By early April, all production came to a halt. Papers were burned, and key managers and scientists ordered to make their way to Oberammergau in Upper Bavaria. Albin Sawatzki, disobeying an SS order to blow up the Mittelwerk factory, stayed behind determined to hand over the complex, of which he was so proud, to the Americans.

On April 3/4, and again the following night, RAF bombers bombed Nordhausen, destroying half the town and killing some 8,800 people, both locals and German refugees and slave workers. Hardest hit was the Boelcke-Kaserne, where some 450 camp inmates were killed in the first raid and 1,000 in the second.

Meanwhile, SS-Sturmbannführer Richard Baer, who had succeeded Otto Förschner as commander of 'Dora' on February 1, had begun preparing the evacuation of all 40,000 inmates then still in the Mittelbau area. When Baer

On the nights of April 3/4 and 4/5, the barracks were hard hit when the RAF bombed Nordhausen town, and over 1,450 inmates were killed. When, six days later, US ground forces reached Nordhausen, they found the starved, emaciated survivors among the mangled corpses of the dead and dying. Many of the dead had succumbed to hunger, exhaustion or maltreatment. Others had been machine-gunned by the SS guards when they attempted to run for cover during the air raids. However, the awkward fact that most of the dead found at the Boelcke were victims of Allied bombing rather than of SS killings was played down or left unsaid in the contemporary accounts – the caption to this photo by Signal Corps photographer, Tech/4 James E. Myers for instance just says that they 'died of starvation or were shot by Gestapo men'. (USNA)

Today, a huge industrial complex covers the site of the Boelcke Barracks, and only a few of the original buildings survive. (Karel Margry)

was wounded in a car crash shortly after, his deputy, SS-Hauptsturmführer Franz Hössler, took over. Between April 4 and 7, all camps were emptied: inmates from 'Dora', Ellrich, Woffleben and the sick from Harzungen by train to destinations in northern Germany (Bergen-Belsen, Sachsenhausen, Ravensbrück); those from Harzungen, Rottleberode, Ilfeld and from camps BB3 and BB4 on foot to the north and east. Many were still to die, from exhaustion or shot by SS guards. One group of over 1,000 prisoners was locked in a barn near Gardelegen and burned alive.

In the days after, the local authorities around Nordhausen used the now-vacated secret weapons factory to shelter some 15,000 civilians, including several hundred patients from the town hospital.

On the morning of April 11, Combat Command B of the US 3rd Armored Division occupied Nordhausen, finding 405 emaciated prisoners surviving among the dead and debris at the Boelcke-Kaserne. The underground factory was only discovered in the late afternoon, by another CCB task force which approached the Kohnstein from the direction of Ellrich. Entering through the northern entrance, the American GIs were completely surprised to find a huge and completely intact bomb-proof factory. Soon, they were led to the camp near the southern exit, where they found some 700 weak inmates who had been left behind in the sick bays, and the corpses of those who had not been burned. The medical troops of the 3rd Armored, and of the 104th Infantry Division which followed them, began immediate relief of the survivors, transferring them to emergency hospitals set up on Nordhausen airfield. Male citizens of Nordhausen were rounded up and ordered to carry the litter cases and corpses, and dug mass graves on a prominent hill outside the town. In all, of some 60,000 prisoners sent to 'Mittelbau-Dora' between 1943 and 1945, an estimated 20,000 – one-third – had perished there.

Troops of both the 3rd Armored Division and the 104th Infantry Division, who arrived in their wake, helped in the relief of the Boelcke Barracks. Sergeant Ragene Ferris of the 329th Medical Battalion, 104th Infantry Division, testified: 'We were battle-tired and combat-wise medics and we thought there was nothing left in the books we didn't know. Yet in a short period of two days, I and many others of the division saw and lived a story we shall never forget. We dismounted, litters in hand, and started for the nearest building with a sense of morbid anxiety. It was a sharp sting of reality which met us at the first doorway. Bombs had ground flesh and bones into the cement floor. Rows upon rows of skin-covered skeletons met our eyes. Men lay as they had starved, discoloured, and lying in indescribable human filth. Their striped coats and prison numbers hung as a last token or symbol of those who enslaved and killed them. In this large motor shop there were no living beings; only the distorted dead. We went to the stairs and under the casing were neatly piled about 75 bodies, a sight I could never erase from my memories.' (NIOD)

Sergeant Ferris: 'Dying on the second floor were, upon later count, about 25 men or half-men. Some of these, lying in double-decked wooden bedsteads, were grotesque yet hanging tenaciously to life's breath. They were still alive.' (NIOD)

A 3rd Armored Division soldier talks to a group of French political prisoners. Although the distinction is rarely made, American eyewitness accounts of 'Nordhausen concentration camp' usually describe the Boelcke-Kaserne rather than 'Dora'. (NIOD)

To speed up relief, Lieutenant Colonel Hugh W. Jones, the 104th Division chief surgeon, and Captain George L. Steinbeck, chaplain of the 329th Medical Battalion, who spoke German, had about 100 male citizens of Nordhausen rounded up to clear away the rubble, act as litter-bearers and bury the dead. (USNA)

The industrial site is a closed area, but a memorial to the victims of the sub-camp and the bombing stands at the factory gate ([1] on the plan on page 74). (Karel Margry)

The dead from the Boelcke were buried in mass graves dug by German civilians in a field opposite the communal cemetery, on a hillside overlooking Nordhausen, about two kilometres from the Boelcke Barracks, and on the same side of town. Picture taken by US Army photographer Pfc John R. Briza on April 14. (USNA)

Looking back to the entrance of what is now the KZ-Ehrenfriedhof (Concentration Camp Cemetery of Honour) on Stresemannring, with the Hauptfriedhof beyond. (Karel Margry)

THE HUNT FOR SECRET WEAPONS AND GERMAN SCIENTISTS

In the days after, numerous Intelligence teams of the US Army, Air Force and Navy inspected the underground facilities and questioned every German specialist whom they managed to find. The most active team was one led by Major Robert B. Staver of the US Office of Scientific Research and Development. Another was the USAAF's Strategic Bombing Survey team. Also, from May 5-22, a British research commission, SHAEF's Central Intelligence Sub-Committee (CIOS) Team No. 163 led by Colonel W. R. J. Cook, made a thorough inspection, not just of the Kohnstein complex but of all the other underground construction projects and secret objects in the Mittelbau area.

Nordhausen was in the Russian zone of occupation as agreed on at the Yalta Conference, and officially the western Allies were not allowed to remove any industrial machinery, equipment, or scientific information from it. However, between April 11 and May 6, Major Staver, who was mainly interested in rockets, had numerous completed V2s and all complete specimens of the Taifun (P), Hs 117, Hs 298, X4 and X7 missiles, together with every document and blueprint his men could find, packed in crates and sent via US Ninth Army G-2 to Paris. From what was left, the British in turn had their pick, removing individual components of the V2 rocket and C2 missile and various radio and navigational apparatus. Another catch was the Peenemünde scientific archives. After a long search, Staver finally found the ten tons of crated documents around the middle of May in the deserted 'Georg-Friedrich' iron-ore mine at Dörnten near Goslar, where a special squad of von Braun's men had buried them in early April. And just before the Russians moved in, Major James P. Hamill of the US Technical Information Mission in Europe removed enough of the half-finished V2s found left on the assembly line in Tunnel B plus component parts, shipping them from Antwerp to New Orleans, to enable the Americans to later assemble 100 rockets from them.

On July 1, 1945, the Americans handed the Nordhausen area over to the Russians. Despite repeated requests by many of the captured German managers and scientists not to let the secret factory fall in Soviet hands intact, the Americans had refused to destroy it. The first Russians to find the tunnel complex were a four-man team under Lieutenant-Colonel Vladimir Shabinsky, who had come to inspect the Niedersachswerfen cement factory and only came upon the underground factory by chance. Although no assembled rockets were left and all scientific papers and major scientists had been removed, the Russians found an intact assembly line, masses of component parts and enough knowledgeable lower-echelon personnel to enable them to again start up production of V2 rockets at Nordhausen itself. To seduce the German engineers, foremen and craftsmen into cooperating, the Russians offered them good houses, high wages and plenty of food and clothing for them and their families. They even managed to secretly lure technicians in the western zones back to the Russian zone.

While the rest of the underground factory was systematically dismantled

and shipped off to the Soviet Union, a part of the assembly line was moved to the buildings of the salt mine at Kleinbodungen, which had previously served as Mittelwerk repair workshops, and a special 'rocket reconstruction office' set up at Bleicherode. The whole project was directed by a Technical Special Commission, led by General Kutshnik (later General Gaidukov) with headquarters at Nordhausen. The new rocket factory, known as the 'Central Works', was led by Hellmut Gröttrup, who had been one of von Braun's electric equipment specialists. Between August 1945 and October 1946, the German and Soviet technicians first reconstructed, then built A4 rockets. Components no longer available were simply ordered anew at the supplier (some orders even being placed in the western zones, the components being secretly smuggled out!). Test firings were conducted at Lehesten in Thuringia, where there had been a factory producing liquid oxygen for V2s, and later at Peenemünde.

However, the German technicians were in for a surprise. On October 22, 1946, Red Army units sealed off Bleicherode and announced the forced 'evacuation' of all German specialists and their families, some 2,000 people in all, to the Soviet Union. Everyone and everything was loaded on a special train which left Kleinbodungen on the 25th for Moscow. Most would come to work at the ballistics research station on the island of Gorodomlia in Lake Seliger, 300 kilometres north-west of Moscow, there to develop the Soviet R10 and R14 rockets before being gradually allowed to return to Germany in 1950-55.

Digging the grave pits and filling them with corpses took several days. (USNA)

By April 18. when Signal Corps photographer Zwick took this picture, the mass graves had been landscaped. The view is south, towards the Boelcke Barracks (indiscernible in the far distance on the left). The main road leading into town in mid-distance is the Hallesche Strasse. (USNA)

Today, grass covers the mass graves and trees hide the view of Nordhausen. (Karel Margry)

On the same day it liberated the Boelcke Barracks, the 3rd Armored Division also discovered 'Dora'. Most of the 10,000-odd inmates had been marched out by the SS the week before, and the Americans found only a few hundred inmates who had been left behind in the camp sick-bay. On May 1, the US Congressional Committee investigating Nazi atrocities (which we saw inspecting a V2 on page 51) made a tour of the camp. Here they are seen walking up the central Lagerstrasse (Camp Road). The hut in the centre is Block 34, the storehouse, with the high fence of the camp sportsground sticking out beyond. Up on the far right is the camp prison. One Congressman said of the SS: 'They reached depth of human degradation beyond belief and constituted no less than organised crime against the civilisation and humanity for which swift, certain and adequate punishment should be meted out to all those who were responsible.' (USNA)

The huts have gone but the Lagerstrasse remains as before.
(Karel Margry)

On June 6, 1945, another American delegation, this time of the American Legion, toured the camp. Here, their cars are just passing the entrance to Tunnel B (away on the right). Beyond the concrete mixer and the V2 fuel tanks are the huts and buildings of the SS compound. On the left lie V2 half-sections, the cones of the rocket's apparatus compartment and more fuel tanks. (USNA)

The two pairs of gate posts make for an easy comparison. (Karel Margry)

The curve of the camp road helps to pinpoint the spot. (Karel Margry)

Outside the camp, the Allies found large quantities of V1 and V2 parts, stored in the open for lack of space inside the mountain. These V2 tail units are along the road just before the entrance to Tunnel A (the turn-off can be seen on the right). The box-car train in the background stands on one of Tunnel A's rail tracks. (BA)

Right on the line of the train track now stands the wagon commemorating the prisoners who died during the harsh train journeys to and from 'Dora'. (Karel Margry)

Two liberated slave labourers pose for Signal Corps photographer Pfc John Briza beside a V2 tail unit. (USNA)

More V2 tail units, these ones packed in transport frames, parked behind the welding shop (Schweisshalle – see the plan on pages 28-29) outside Tunnel A. The camouflage of the tunnel entrance can be seen on the right. Compare with the pictures on page 16. (USNA)

Almost on the same spot, rows of V2 combustion units and, partly under canvas, V2 apparatus compartments. The welding shop is visible on the left. (USNA)

Of course, the secret underground factory, captured completely intact, attracted much attention from Anglo-American scientific intelligence teams. Though bound by the Yalta agreement not to remove anything, the Allies carried off a large number of V2s, experimental missiles and tons of scientific papers before the Russians arrived in July. Here, a US Jeep is seen leaving Tunnel B. Compare with the pictures on page 14. (NIOD)

One of the units helping SHAEF's scientific Team No. 163 to remove hardware from Nordhausen was the 1680th Artillery Platoon, RASC. They arrived on June 5 with 26 3-ton trucks. In addition to loading several trains, they despatched four vehicles loaded with 'special equipment' to Brussels by road on the 14th, leaving themselves on the 19th. Lance Corporal John Pike pictured one of the platoon's Bedfords along the Mittelwerk railway. (via Percy Upton)

This snapshot, taken by Driver Rich Edwards, shows two of the platoon's trucks near the entrance to Tunnel B. (via Percy Upton)

Tunnel B pictured by a member of the British research team in May 1945. The train is probably one of those used by them to remove V-weapon parts from the factory. Note that the watchtower above the entrance has now collapsed. (BA)

Like the Americans, the British thoroughly explored all the various underground facilities before the area was surrendered to the Russians. These are the tunnel entrances of B-11 at Niedersachswerfen, pictured by John Pike of 1680th Platoon. (via Percy Upton)

Summer 1948: the Soviet occupation army closes the Kohnstein tunnel system with demolitions. Picture by H. Beikirch from the Johannisberg hill. (Gedenkstätte Mittelbau-Dora)

AFTERMATH

The complete dismantling of the Mittelwerk complex took till the spring of 1948. That summer, the Soviets filled the underground factory with explosives and tried to blow it up. The detonation failed to produce the desired result, so they sealed the tunnels by blowing up the entrances.

After liberation, camp 'Dora' was used by the Americans as a Displaced Persons camp. In August 1945 and a few weeks after, the Russians used it to intern former Nazis. From November, it housed German refugees, mainly Sudeten Germans driven out from Czechoslovakia. Dissolved in August 1946, the camp was broken up and all the huts, guard towers and the camp fence were pulled down.

A 'Dora' war crimes trial was held before a US Military Court at Dachau in 1947. On trial stood only one civilian, General Director Georg Rickhey (who was acquitted), and 18 SS officers and guards. After that, the records of the trial and the preceding investigation were classified and would remain secret for over 30 years. This was to suppress the embarrassing truth that some of the German scientists whom the Americans had brought to the US and who were to pioneer the American space programme – men like Arthur Rudolph, Mittelwerk's plant manager and chief clerk, and later project director of NASA's Saturn 5 project – had been closely involved with 'Mittelbau-Dora'. (Rudolph only came up for prosecution in 1978 after US President Jimmy Carter had created the Office of Special Investigation to prosecute Nazi war

The memorial wall erected beside the Appellplatz in GDR times. (Karel Margry)

criminals living in the US; in 1983, before he could be charged, Rudolph relinquished US citizenship and returned to Germany. He died in 1996.)

In the post-war world, Nordhausen and the Kohnstein became part of East Germany (GDR, German Democratic Republic). The 'Dora' camp site was made a memorial by the local GDR authorities, the area around the crematorium being landscaped and a bronze sculpture being dedicated in front of it in 1964. In 1973, the site became an official GDR Mahn- und Gedenkstätte (Remembrance and Memorial Site) and a museum exhibition was opened in the crematorium building. Many state-organised, anti-Fascist mass meetings were held here, but few people from the West managed to visit it. (When After the Battle first asked to visit and photograph the site back in 1973, the request was refused on the grounds that the location was 'a border area'.)

For over four decades, the underground tunnels of the Mittelwerk remained inaccessible (except for the occasional adventurous souvenir-hunter who illegally and riskily climbed down the air shafts). Only Tunnels C and D (of the never-finished project B-12) on the north-east side of the Kohnstein were re-opened in 1965-66 and made into cold-storage warehouses for vegetables and

The new tunnel, dug in 1988-95 to enable visitors to enter Tunnel A. (Karel Margry)

V2 'T-Stoff' container recovered from the Kohnstein and now at the Memorial museum.
(Karel Margry)

fruit. Meanwhile, the gypsum quarry at Niedersachswerfen, restarted by the Russians in 1945 and continued as the Leuna-Werke 'Walther Ulbricht' by the GDR since 1953, nibbled away at the Kohnstein. By 1990, quarrying had taken away nearly all of what had once been project B-11 and almost reached Tunnel A between galleries 40-44.

With the German reunification of 1990, the Gedenkstätte Mittelbau-Dora, like the other camp memorials in the former GDR, was faced with a thorough reorganisation and overhaul of its conception. Meanwhile, the threat to the tunnel system grew as the gypsum factory, now taken over by a West-German owner, accelerated quarrying even more. It was only lifted in June 1991, when the state of Thuringia declared the tunnels a protected historical site. In 1992, the exhibition in the crematorium was removed, both because it was too one-sided and in order to restore the building's authentic appearance. Since 1991, large parts of the actual camp, which the GDR authorities had allowed to disappear under bushes and trees, were cleared, laying bare the foundations of nearly every hut and building. On one of these, an original camp hut was rebuilt; this was used to house a

In April 1995, a spectacular recovery operation took place when a complete turbo section of a V2, which had been located the previous September, was raised from the water in Gallery 29 to be displayed at a special exhibition on Nazi rocket scientists at the Technik-Museum in Berlin. (Technik-Museum Berlin)

new and more-balanced exhibition which was opened on April 11, 1995 – the 50th anniversary of the camp's liberation. Other memorials erected by the GDR were left in place.

At the same time, work was in progress to make at least a part of the underground galleries accessible to visitors. For that purpose, a new 180-metre-long tunnel was dug from just next to the southern entrance to Tunnel B, giving access to a 100-metre stretch of Tunnel A and views of Gallery 46, one of those where in 1943 several thousand inmates subsisted and later V1s were assembled. The tunnels can only be visited as part of conducted tours given by the Memorial staff. In the first year of opening, 1995, there were already over 100,000 visitors. All galleries are in a state of total chaos and destruction – the result of dismantling, demolition and erosion – and partly flooded by ground water. In the dark, damp tunnels, between the debris and rocks, lie the rusty remains of machinery, equipment and the sinister remains of once-secret weapons – macabre memorials to the suffering that took place here.

In September 2006, the Mittelbau-Dora Memorial opened a new permanent exhibition in a new building erected on the southern side of the former camp grounds, between the former camp site and the southern tunnel exits. The building also houses a museum bookshop, offices for the memorial's staff and research department, a library and seminar rooms.

THE GARDELEGEN MASSACRE

ON THE MORNING OF April 15, 1945, soldiers of the 2nd Battalion, 405th Infantry, of the US 102nd Infantry Division were engaged in a routine search of the area around the Luftwaffe airfield at Gardelegen, a small recently-captured town 50 kilometres north-west of Magdeburg in northern Germany, when they discovered evidence of a recent Nazi atrocity. At the top of a small hill overlooking the airfield and the town, they found a big

On April 15, 1945, soldiers of the US 102nd Infantry Division patrolling outside the small German town of Gardelegen discovered the site of what was perhaps the most horrendous of all Nazi atrocities. Two days before, on April 13, SS concentration camp guards and Fallschirmjäger soldiers had locked over a thousand camp prisoners of the Reich in a big barn and set it on fire, throwing in hand-grenades and firing Panzerfaust rounds into the interior. Anyone trying to escape from the burning, smoke-filled building was shot. As a result, a total of 1,016 men died. Although unparalleled in cruelty and horror, the murder action at the Isenschnibbe barn was not an isolated case as there were several other instances of mass shootings of prisoners in the Gardelegen area during the same week. (IWM)

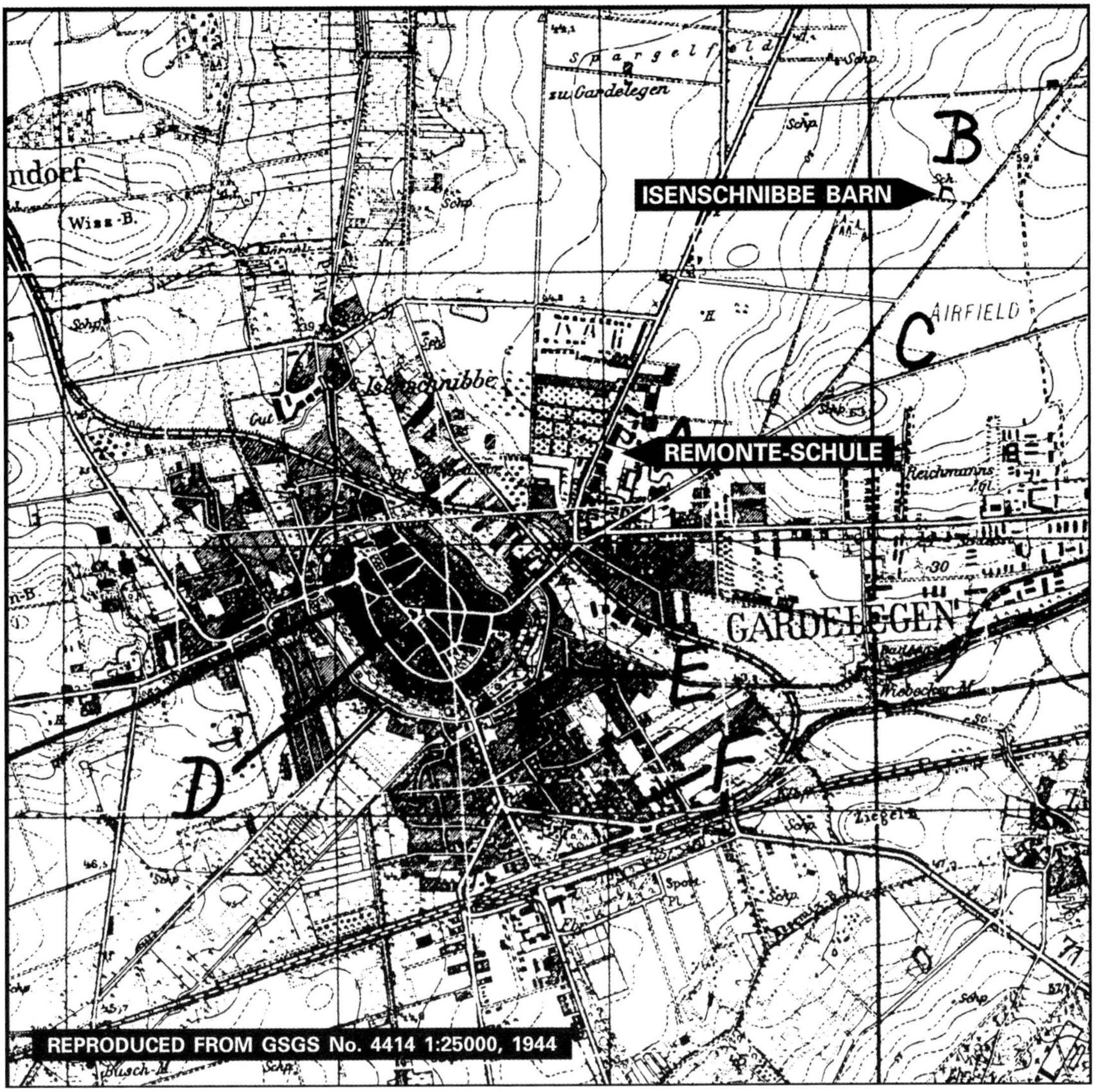

The Isenschnibbe barn stood in open fields just north-east of Gardelegen town. The prisoners marched there from the Remonte-Schule barracks on Bismarker Strasse. This is a contemporary annotated plan from the US War Crimes Investigation Team's file. We have added the position of the school and barn. (NIOD)

masonry harvest-storage barn. Several bodies wearing striped prison garments lay in the green spring wheat nearby, riddled with bullet wounds and showing peculiar burns. Taking a closer look at the barn, the GIs saw five more bodies sprawled through a jagged hole in the brick-work. When one of the barn's great wooden doors was pushed open, there emerged a cloud of smoke and a revolting stench of burned flesh. Overcoming their nausea, the soldiers explored the interior. There they found, heaped in every conceivable contortion of agony and death, the charred and smoking bodies of hundreds of men. The Americans had discovered the site of what would become notorious as the Gardelegen massacre.

The 1,016 unfortunates who were found murdered at the barn at Gardelegen were all inmates of Nazi concentration camps – some of them

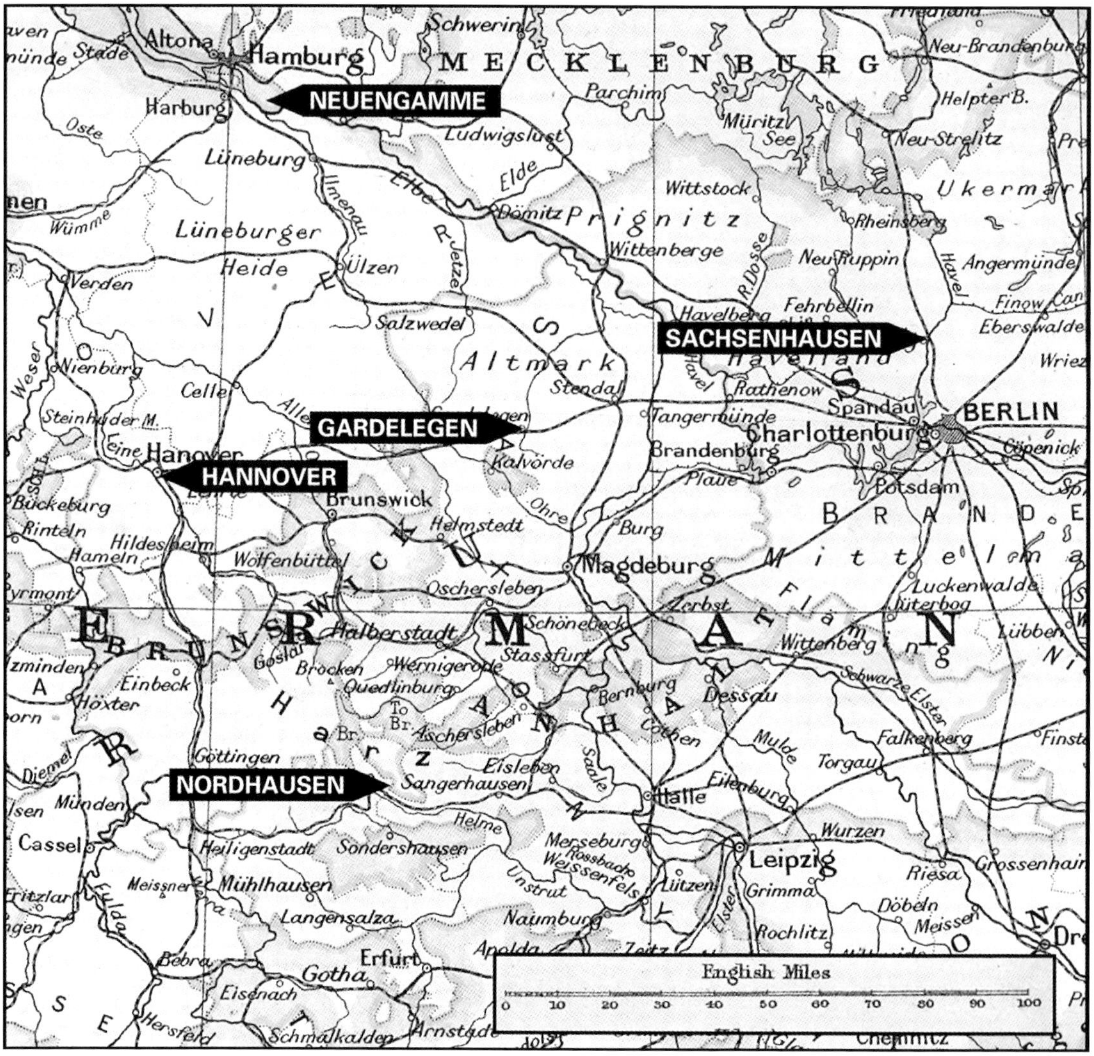

Most of the prisoners murdered at Gardelegen came from slave-labour camps of the 'Mittelbau' complex around Nordhausen, 120 kilometres to the south of Gardelegen, with others coming from Hannover-Stöcken, a sub-camp of Neuengamme, 120 kilometres due west of Gardelegen.

Jews, most of them political prisoners. They had been marched to the barn from the Remonte-Schule (Remount School), an army school for training cavalry horses on Bismarker Strasse in Gardelegen town. Its official name since 1936 was Wehrkreis-Reit- und Fahrschule (Military District Riding and Driving School). The Remonte-Schule barracks was itself no concentration camp but had only become a reception centre for wandering groups of camp prisoners in the few days preceding the massacre. These prisoners had arrived in the Gardelegen area by train at two different places: Letzlingen, 12 kilometres south-east of Gardelegen, and Mieste, 12 kilometres west of the town. For clarity, it is best to follow the events as they unfolded at each of these arrival points in turn, but first we must describe the general background that led up to the massacre.

In early 1945, faced with the unstoppable advance of the Soviet army on the Eastern front, the Germans began evacuating the concentration and extermination camps in the East. In exhausting foot-marches the starved and weakened inmates were driven westwards. Those unable to keep up the march tempo were ruthlessly shot by their SS guards, their bodies left by the wayside. The aimed destination of these 'death marches' were the concentration camps in central Germany, mostly Bergen-Belsen, Neuengamme, Ravensbrück, Sachsenhausen, Dachau and Mauthausen. However, as the Allied advance from East and West continued, many camps inside Germany itself became threatened too, and their inmates were hurriedly moved off in turn on foot or by rail to other destinations.

One of the installations evacuated in early April 1945 was 'Dora-Mittelbau'. Preparation for the evacuation of the 40,000 inmates then surviving in the 'Dora' main camp and its various satellite camps began on April 1. Between April 4 and 7, all camps were emptied, groups of inmates departing by train to destinations in northern Germany – Bergen-Belsen, Neuengamme, Sachsenhausen, Ravensbrück – or marching out to the north and east.

The Letzlingen train

The first of the 'Mittelbau' evacuations that would end up at Gardelegen consisted of the inmates of the small satellite camps at Wieda, Osterhagen, Nüxei and Mackenrode, housing the slave workers of SS-Bau-Brigade 3. On April 6, the men from the latter three camps were first marched to Wieda. From there, on the 7th the assembled prisoners, numbering about 1,135, set off northwards through the Harz mountains, in two march groups of 400; the 335 men too sick to walk were put on a narrow-gauge train. The walking groups spent the first night together under the open sky in an open field in the forest between Braunlage and Elend, the second night in an empty labour camp at Wernigerode and in a small munitions factory just before that town respectively. Here they were reunited with the sick inmates who had travelled there by rail. On the morning of the 9th, the whole group of 1,130 was put on a train consisting of closed freight cars which set out from Wernigerode northwards. So far, the evacuation had been led by SS-Untersturmführer (2nd Lieutenant) Kurt Merkle, the deputy commander of SS-Bau-Brigade 3, but he left at Wernigerode, leaving SS-Stabscharführer (Staff Sergeant) Kemnitz as Transportführer (convoy commander).

The train made a wide detour to the north-west, making long stops at various stations and stopping for the night at Jerxheim. Late on the 10th it reached the western suburbs of Magdeburg, which had just suffered an Allied air raid and where Allied fighter-bombers strafed the train. American ground forces were already in the southern outskirts, and all Elbe bridges in the city had been blown, so the train had no option but to go north. Continuing via secondary lines through Gross-Ammensleben, Neuhaldensleben and Wannefeld/Roxförde, at around 1730 hours on the 11th the train rolled into

The small station of Letzlingen, 12 kilometres south-east of Gardelegen, where the train evacuating about 1,100 slave workers from the 'Mittelbau' camps of Wieda, Osterhagen, Nüxei and Mackenrode came to a halt on April 11. The SS guards, indecisive on what to do next, first allowed the prisoners to run away, then opened fire on them with automatic weapons. Most of the survivors were rounded up, with a total of about 185 being marched to Gardelegen, some of which would end up in the murder barn two days later. Few of the survivors from this train knew the name of the station where their rail journey had ended. Hence, Letzlingen was hardly mentioned in any of the survivor statements collected by the US Army war crimes investigators after the atrocity. Some survivors thought they had alighted at Zienau, a station on the main Hannover-Berlin line three kilometres south-east of Gardelegen; others mentioned a place called Ortschen or Ochen; some – probably because they had heard where the other train had stopped – even named Mieste. Only one man named Letzlingen. In their final report, the US investigators concluded the train had stopped at Zienau. Although this was mistaken, the name stuck and many historians since have said that at least some of the atrocity victims came from the station there. The Letzlingen line was lifted in the 1970s, and the station now lies disused. (Karel Margry)

the small station outside the village of Letzlingen, 12 kilometres south-east of Gardelegen.

The train was shunted on to a side track, its last wagon – carrying the convoy kitchen, food supplies and the luggage and bicycles of the SS guards – was unhinged, moved to another line, and unloaded. Artillery fire of the approaching Americans could be heard in the distance. Clearly the SS were deliberating what to do next. Transportführer Kemnitz was overheard saying: 'What shall we do with them? Let them go or shoot them?' Several of his men took the opportunity to change into civilian clothes and take off.

Shortly after, there occurred a confusing situation when Allied fighter-bombers passed over the train at low level. Apparently, Transportführer Kemnitz told some of the prisoners to run away and this, combined with

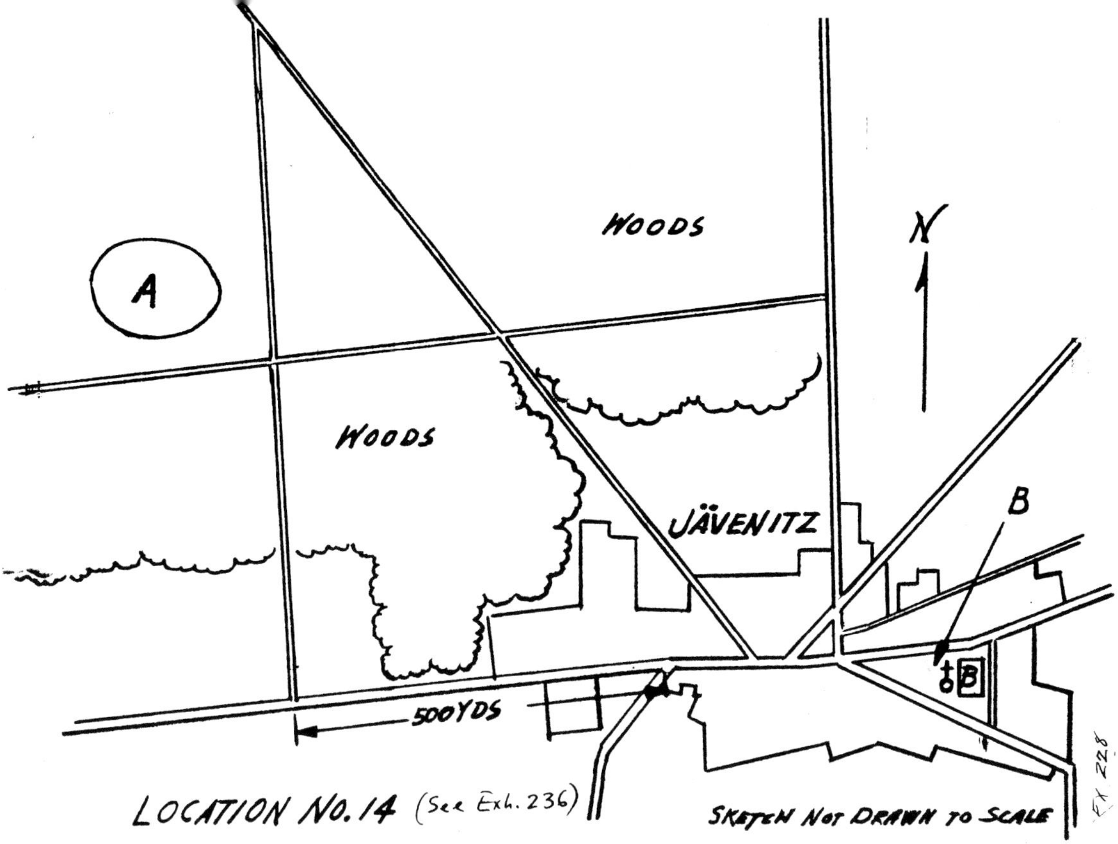

A group of 125 prisoners from the Letzlingen train was marched out of Gardelegen eastward early on the 12th. Next morning, April 13, two SS men and two Luftwaffe soldiers led them into a wood just west of the village of Jävenitz and opened fire on them, killing 31. They were buried in 17 makeshift graves. This sketch showing the site of the murder action and graves [A] comes from the file on the Gardelegen case prepared by the US Ninth Army's war crimes investigators in April-May 1945. (NIOD)

the panic caused by the air attack, resulted in a mass escape by the prisoners. Throwing open the unlocked doors, hundreds of men jumped from the wagons and ran off, most of them towards the woods to the west. They had not gone far when the SS guards opened fire on them with machine pistols and mowed down a great many of them. Of those that kept running, a few made good their escape, but many were recaptured, not a few being shot on the spot. (The bodies of 33 prisoners were later found at Letzlingen, ten at Wannefeld, and another 23 at Roxförde.) About 165-185 were surrounded and rounded up by Luftwaffe soldiers at Neue Mühle near the hamlet of Polvitz, five kilometres to the north-west. They were marched off to Gardelegen, a first group of 125 setting out at 2130 hours and arriving at the Remonte School before midnight. A second group of 40-60 left after midnight, reaching the Remonte-Schule at 0700 on the 12th.

The spot in the woods where the prisoners were murdered and buried. (Karel Margry)

The 31 victims of the massacre in the woods were recovered by the US Army on May 13, 1945, and re-interred at the Jävenitz village cemetery – [B] on the sketch. The recovery and reburial was supervised by Captain Luther E. Gowder and a detail of the 381st Field Artillery Battalion of the 102nd Division. Picture taken by Army photographer Tech/5 Philip R. Mark of the 168th Signal Photographic Company. (NIOD)

The Jävenitz cemetery today. The individual crosses have gone and the memorial on the grave plot, placed there in GDR times, states the number of dead buried there as 28. (Karel Margry)

Of these two groups from Letzlingen, only the second one would end up as a victim of the Gardelegen massacre. The first contingent of 125 would narrowly escape it. Early on the 12th, about the time that the other group came in, they were marched off again, towards the east. They spent the night in a big farm barn near the village of Jävenitz, seven kilometres on from Gardelegen. Next morning, April 13, the group was taken into the forest. There arrived two SS-Unterscharführers with two Luftwaffe soldiers, who ordered the ethnic Germans among the prisoners to step aside, and then opened fire with machine pistols on the remainder, killing 31. The others made a run for it, scattering in the surrounding woods. Armed parties of Volkssturm (home guard) and Hitlerjugend teenagers began a man-hunt of the area, searching farms and woods for the escapees. Four men were shot by a Hitlerjugend boy at the neighbouring village of Hottendorf. By noon, most of the fugitives, about 96, had been recaptured and assembled at Jävenitz.

At 1930, an order arrived that these prisoners were to be taken back to Gardelegen. Luftwaffe soldiers quick-marched them to the airfield there, but by the time they arrived, about 2000 hours, smoke was already billowing up from the massacre barn on the horizon, and they were told to return to Jävenitz. Later that night, Erich Matthies, a civilian who owned a tractor with two trailers, was told to bring the prisoners to the Remonte-Schule. He left at midnight, but when he reached the barracks, it was empty of prisoners and the sentries at the gate told him: 'You have come too late. We don't want any prisoners'. Matthies took the 96 men in his custody back to Jävenitz. The burgomaster, Fritz Matthies (Erich's brother), hid them in a barn near the village for two days, providing them with hot food and coffee. On April 15, the 96 were liberated there by the Americans.

After the mass escape and the subsequent round-up, there remained some 700 prisoners at the Letzlingen railway station, guarded by the few remaining SS guards and by Volkssturm men. Most of them never got near Gardelegen, but were marched off the following morning (April 12) in the general direction of the Elbe. One small group of only 30 marched south-east towards Colbitz, 15 kilometres away, where they were liberated by troops of the US 30th Division on the 13th.

A much larger group of some 570 set off along a secondary road due east. Convoy commander Kemnitz had requisitioned 16 trucks and horse-drawn carts from the local population to carry the sick and invalid. They brought them as far as Dolle, the first next village ten kilometres on. From there, all were required to walk. Some 66 prisoners were killed, those too feeble to walk being shot by the guards and others, caught escapees, being clubbed to death by civilians. The rest marched on to the next village, Burgstall, where they camped for the night. Here the NSDAP-Ortsgruppenleiter (Nazi party local leader), Kurt Möhring, and a local lawyer, Hermann Prett, prevented the guards from another mass shooting by producing a fake 'counter-order'. Thus saved, this group of 500 was liberated by troops of the US 35th Division that afternoon, April 13.

Yet a third group, about 100 strong, set off due east, guarded by SS and armed Kapos (prisoners with authority over other prisoners). They actually crossed the Elbe river in small boats, marching on to the town of Brandenburg and then north-east, aiming for Sachsenhausen. During their two-week trek, about half of them died of exhaustion or were shot by the guards. Others managed to escape, the lucky ones being finally liberated by the Soviet Army in the last days of April.

The Mieste train

The second Nordhausen group to end up at Gardelegen was made up of inmates from the 'Mittelbau' satellite camps Rottleberode, Stempeda, Ilfeld and Ellrich, with inmates from Nordhausen's main camp 'Dora' and a few stragglers from one or two other camps being added in.

On the evening of April 4, some 1,500 inmates of Rottleberode and nearby Stempeda were assembled and marched off to the railway station

Mieste station, 12 kilometres west of Gardelegen, end of rail journey for some 1,400 inmates evacuated from the 'Mittelbau' camps of Rottleberode, Stempeda, Ilfeld and Ellrich, and for the 300-400 living skeletons evacuated from the Hannover-Stöcken sick bay. Their respective trains arrived at Mieste shortly after one another on April 9. After languishing in the railway yard for nearly three days, and with the American army coming ever nearer, the prisoners were marched away to the east on the 11th, most of them to meet their end in the murder barn at Gardelegen. Army photographer Tech/5 Philip R. Mark took these pictures of the abandoned evacuation trains on May 11, precisely a month to the day after the death march from the station began. The prisoners' train is the one on the track closest to the camera. On the left is the cement factory where turnip soup was handed out to the starved prisoners on the second day – for many their only meal in over a week. (NIOD)

The same view today. The new tracks for the Intercity Express super-fast train were added in the 1990s.
(Karel Margry)

A further 17 boxcars stood abandoned just east of the level crossing, as shown in this shot looking the other way. There is still some un-clarity about how many prisoner evacuation trains ended up stranded at Mieste. There is no doubt about the one from 'Mittelbau' and the one from Hannover-Stöcken. The former had about 20 waggons, and the latter eight, making a total of 28. However, the American sketch (see page 112) indicates a total of 54 boxcars in the station. The additional cars may well have arrived with other cargo (some of the cars on the right-hand track in the previous shot certainly look like they carried ordinary freight), or after the prisoners left, but they also leave the possibility that other prisoner transports did end up in Mieste as well. Some accounts mention a train with inmates from Neuengamme arriving on the night of April 10/11, but there is nothing in the survivor testimonies to substantiate this. (NIOD)

Looking east from Mieste railway station today. (Karel Margry)

of Niedersachswerfen, 18 kilometres away. They left in two groups – one of 400 led by the Lagerführer (deputy camp commander) of Rottleberode, SS-Hauptscharführer (Sergeant Major) Erhard Brauny, and one of 1,100 led by the camp commander of Stempeda, SS-Unterscharführer Hermann Lamp. It was a harsh night march, in cold rain and over the muddy slippery roads of the Harz foothills.

Brauny's group of 400 reached Niedersachswerfen on the morning of the 5th, but the prisoners had to wait until afternoon before a train became available for them. It was made up of some 15 open boxcars, of which ten turned out to be already filled with some 600 inmates from other 'Mittelbau' camps: 300 from Ilfeld, the rest perhaps from main camp 'Dora', perhaps from the overflow camp at the Boelcke Barracks in Nordhausen town.

The 300 Ilfeld inmates had left their camp on foot at 0900 that morning led by the deputy camp commander, SS-Unterscharführer (Sergeant) Hermann Rose, and had reached Niedersachswerfen, six kilometres on, at 1030. They were kept separate from the inmates of other camps, being loaded in six cars: one for their 13 SS guards, one for the baggage and four for the prisoners.

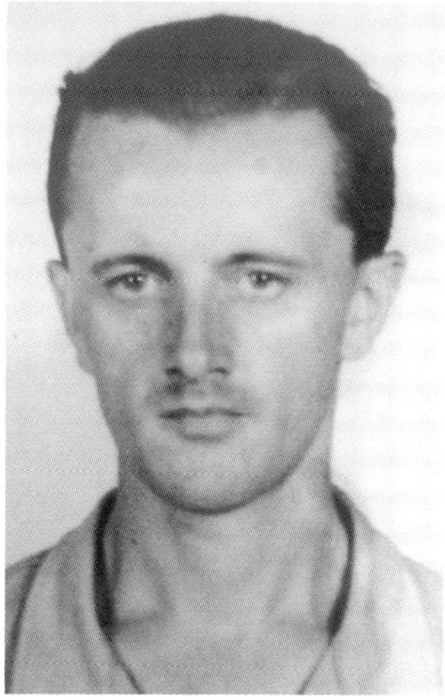

The man in charge at Mieste was SS-Hauptscharführer Erhard Brauny, the senior convoy commander of the 'Mittelbau' train. Born on October 17, 1913, Brauny had joined the Hitlerjugend in 1930 and become a member of both the NSDAP and the SS in 1932. In September 1939 he was posted to Buchenwald camp, becoming a Kommandoführer at the Tondorf-Erfurt sub-camp in January 1940, and guard leader at the Cologne sub-camp in August 1941. In August 1943, he was assigned to camp 'Dora' at Nordhausen, where he served as roll-call leader and block leader. In November 1944, he became deputy commander of the Rottleberode sub-camp. In all of these positions, he gained a terrible reputation for beating, killing and starving prisoners. On April 4, 1945, he led the evacuation of Rottleberode, beginning an odyssey that would bring the inmates to Mieste, and eventually to death in Gardelegen. (Gedenkstätte Mittelbau-Dora)

Brauny's 400 were ordered to climb aboard the remaining six cars, but the train did not leave as Brauny waited all day for the other Rottleberode column to arrive. Finally, driving back there on a motorcycle, Brauny learned that Lamp's group had taken another route. He decided to go without them, but it was past noon on April 6 before the train finally left Niedersachswerfen. It only drove to Ellrich station, seven kilometres on, where it stopped again.

Late in the evening another five open-topped boxcars were hooked on, and in these, during the night, were loaded some 400 inmates from Ellrich-Bürgergarten, the satellite camp housing slave workers of SS-Bau-Brigade 4: all of the camp's 200 sick inmates, plus 150-200 Jewish prisoners from camp Mackenrode who had been shoved off to Ellrich on March 26. This group was accompanied by 15 guards under SS-Oberscharführer (Quartermaster Sergeant) Locke. A few inmates from Woffleben camp and Russian prisoners from 'Dora' are said to have boarded the train here too.

The whole train, now 20 cars long and carrying some 1,400 prisoners and 100 guards, left Ellrich early on the 7th with Brauny as senior Transportführer. It travelled west to Herzberg, then north to Osterode (some sources say that the 300 Ilfeld inmates boarded the train here, but that is not correct). For food, each prisoner had received a loaf of bread and a small tin of meat paste. To protect their weak, emaciated bodies during the cold ride in open wagons, they had only their thin camp garments and a few blankets. Each car contained 60 to 100 persons. They had no room to sit or lie down and had to sleep on top of each other. During the journey numerous men died from hunger or cold. Their dead bodies lay squeezed among the living in the wagons.

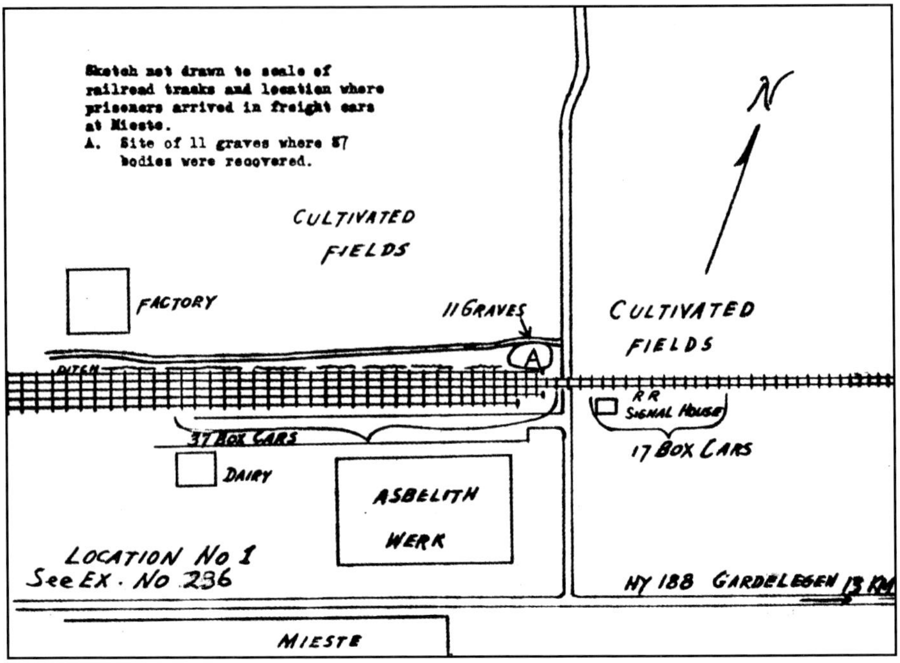

Situation sketch of Mieste station prepared by the US investigators. (NIOD)

Just outside Osterode, at the village of Lasfelde, the train was attacked by American fighter-bombers. The locomotive was heavily damaged and three SS men (the SS from Rottleberode travelled in the wagon behind the locomotive) and five prisoners were killed, and several others wounded. Two Russian prisoners were shot by an SS guard as they tried to open the wagon containing the food. The SS and local medics took care of the German casualties, leaving the prisoners to bury their dead in a common grave beside the track. In the panic caused by the air attack, numerous prisoners jumped from the train but it is not known how many succeeded to flee or how many were shot while doing so. The SS guards, helped by Volkssturm and Hitlerjugend from the village, started rounding them up as soon as the air raid was over.

A new locomotive was arranged and the train continued its journey, only to stop for another air raid alarm at Badenhausen, four kilometres on. No aircraft appeared, but again there were escape attempts, followed by man-hunts, and escapees being shot. After this, the train continued north via Seesen, Salzgitter and Braunschweig to Gifhorn, where it turned east on the main Hannover-Berlin line towards Oebisfelde, where it stopped for the night of April 8/9. (Other sources say it already turned east at Braunschweig, going to Helmstedt, then north again on secondary lines via Marienborn and Weferlingen to Oebisfelde.) Whatever its precise route, the shift to the east was apparently caused by an order which Brauny had received on the 8th to change the train's destination from Neuengamme in northern Germany to a camp in the east, probably Sachsenhausen.

In the early morning of April 9, the train came to a final halt at the railway

About 50-60 prisoners had died from hunger or exhaustion, either during the train journey or during the three days at Mieste. Another 25-30 were murdered by the German guards, either because they had collapsed or were looking for food or because they ran away when Allied aircraft strafed the station on the 12th. Prisoner details buried a total of 86 dead prisoners in a plot beside the level crossing. Directed by Lieutenant Colonel Edward E. Cruise, one of the officers investigating the Gardelegen case, Tech/5 Mark pictured their disinterment on April 11. (NIOD)

The same plot today, now a weed-filled gravel pit. (Karel Margry)

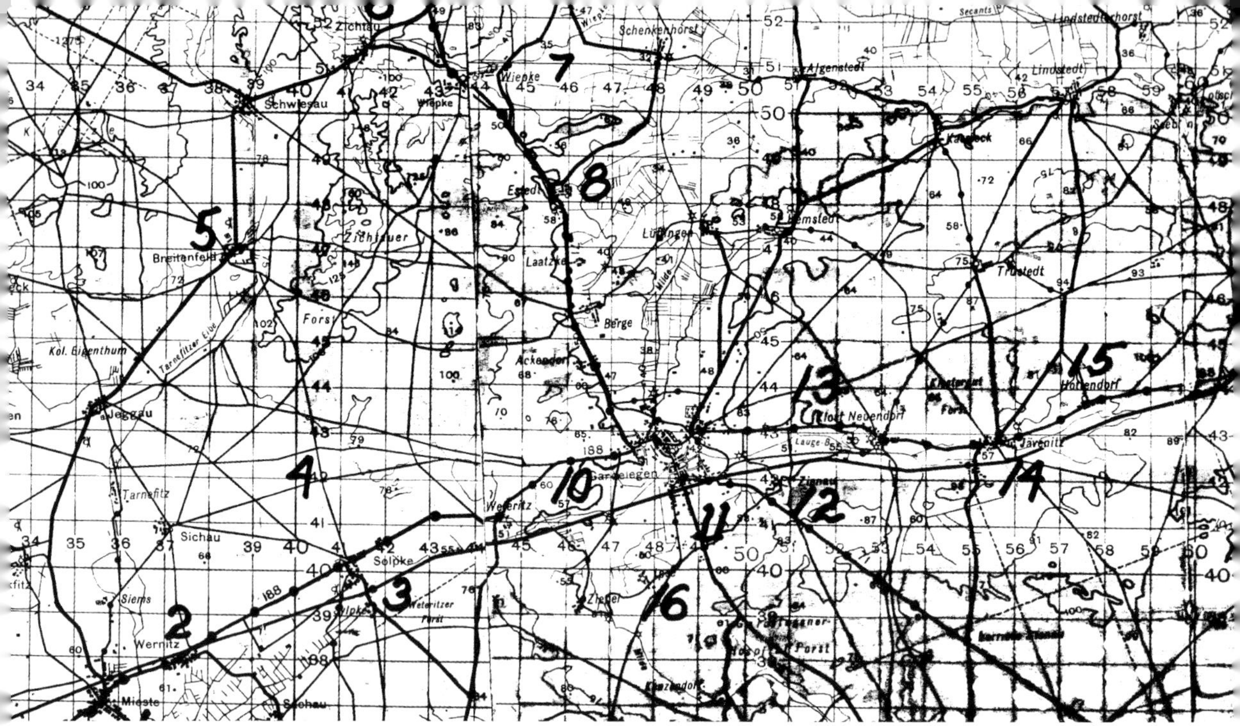

The master map from the US Army war crimes file shows all the major locations around Gardelegen, except Letzlingen. The routes of the death marches from Mieste to Gardelegen can be traced on them as well. [1] Mieste. [2] Wernitz. [3] Solpke. [4] Forest intersection where guards shot 15 prisoners. [5] Breitenfeld. [6] Zichtau. [7] Wiepke. [8] Estedt. [10] Gardelegen. [11] Lindenthal. [12] Zienau. [13] Kloster Neuendorf. [14] Jävenitz. [15] Hottendorf. [16] Ipse. (NIOD)

station at Mieste, 12 kilometres west of Gardelegen, its further journey to Stendal blocked by destruction of the rail tracks at Solpke, six kilometres ahead. (Some sources state that the 300 inmates from Ilfeld already got off at Bergfriede, a station ten kilometres west of Mieste, but this is not correct.) The locomotive was uncoupled and driven off, leaving the train stranded in the railway yard. The three convoy commanders – Brauny from Rottleberode, Rose from Ilfeld, and Locke from Ellrich – conferred on what to do next. Brauny telephoned the SS main office in charge of concentration camps at Sachsenhausen for instructions, but the authorities there apparently told him to make his own decisions.

Shortly after, another prisoner evacuation transport rolled into Mieste – bringing with it the third main group that would end up at Gardelegen. It did not come from 'Dora-Mittelbau' but from the slave labour camp at Hannover-Stöcken, a satellite of Neuengamme concentration camp housing the slave workers for the Accumulatoren-Fabrik AG in Stöcken which produced batteries for U-boats and torpedo engines. The majority of its inmates had left for Bergen-Belsen on the 6th, but 600 sick prisoners had been left behind in the camp hospital. Early on the 8th, they were all perched into eight cattle cars. Many of them suffered from dysentery, quite a few were naked. There was no place for any patient to lie down, no water, and only a few loafs of bread thrown in before departure. The train had no guards and, during a stop in Hannover station, 150 prisoners escaped. At 0600 on the 9th this train reached Mieste station and was shunted behind the 'Mittelbau' train. When its doors were opened, many of the 300-450 men inside were too weak even to crawl out. Several had died on the journey. The SS guards of Brauny's train shot the weaker survivors and took over guarding the others. (When Brauny's train arrived at Mieste there already was another stranded train standing in the station yard but it appears that this was not a prisoner evacuation transport.)

With two prisoner trains stranded at Mieste the combined number of prisoners there now amounted to some 1,500-1,800. By now, the starved prisoners had had nothing to eat for days. Some were lucky to find a few raw potatoes. Others ate grass taken from the railway embankment. The only drinking water was from a ditch alongside the track. Civilians who felt pity for these unfortunates and wanted to give them some bread or milk were reproved by others or chased off by the guards. Burgomaster Adolf Krüger of Mieste refused to distribute food to the prisoners, but on the 10th – on orders of Landrat (region commissioner) Dr Daue – Oberleutnant Fritz Hesse of the Oebisfelde gendarmerie arranged for a meal to be cooked, ordering the supply of 130lb of meat, 2,500lb of potatoes, 1,200lb of turnips and 6lb of coffee. This meal, cooked in the cement factory beside the track and handed out by the guards, was totally inadequate to feed all. Many prisoners were too feeble to be able to stand in the food line. Others fought each other for what food they got, watched by laughing guards. While at Mieste some 60 men succumbed to hunger and thirst, most of them from the Hannover-Stöcken group.

The SS guards left the task of guarding the trains mostly to the Kapos, arming some of them with rifles, while they themselves got drunk in the local cafes. To reinforce the guard, members of the local Volkssturm, Hitlerjugend, and soldiers from Luftwaffe units stationed in the area took up position around the railway yard.

Late on the 9th a group of Luftwaffe soldiers led by a lieutenant shot eight prisoners who wanted to get some corn from a nearby grain storage. Obergefreiter Franz Unverdorben, a guard from Ellrich, killed three prisoners who had collapsed from hunger with a bullet through the head. Even prisoners who wanted to relieve themselves in the cement factory were shot. In all, some 25 men were killed by guards at Mieste. Prisoner details carried the dead to a spot beside the track where they could be buried. A total of 86 bodies was later recovered from here.

On the morning of the 11th, Allied fighter-bombers attacked the train and one bomb fell on the railway yard, causing everyone to scurry in all directions. In the mêlée, some 17 prisoners were shot by the guards, a few managed to escape.

At 1130, Transportführer Brauny received word that the Americans were only 13 kilometres away and rapidly approaching. He ordered that all prisoners be marched off to the east. Before departure, each prisoner received three or four potatoes. The prisoners left in three groups of different size. Those unable to walk, about 200-300, were transported on 21

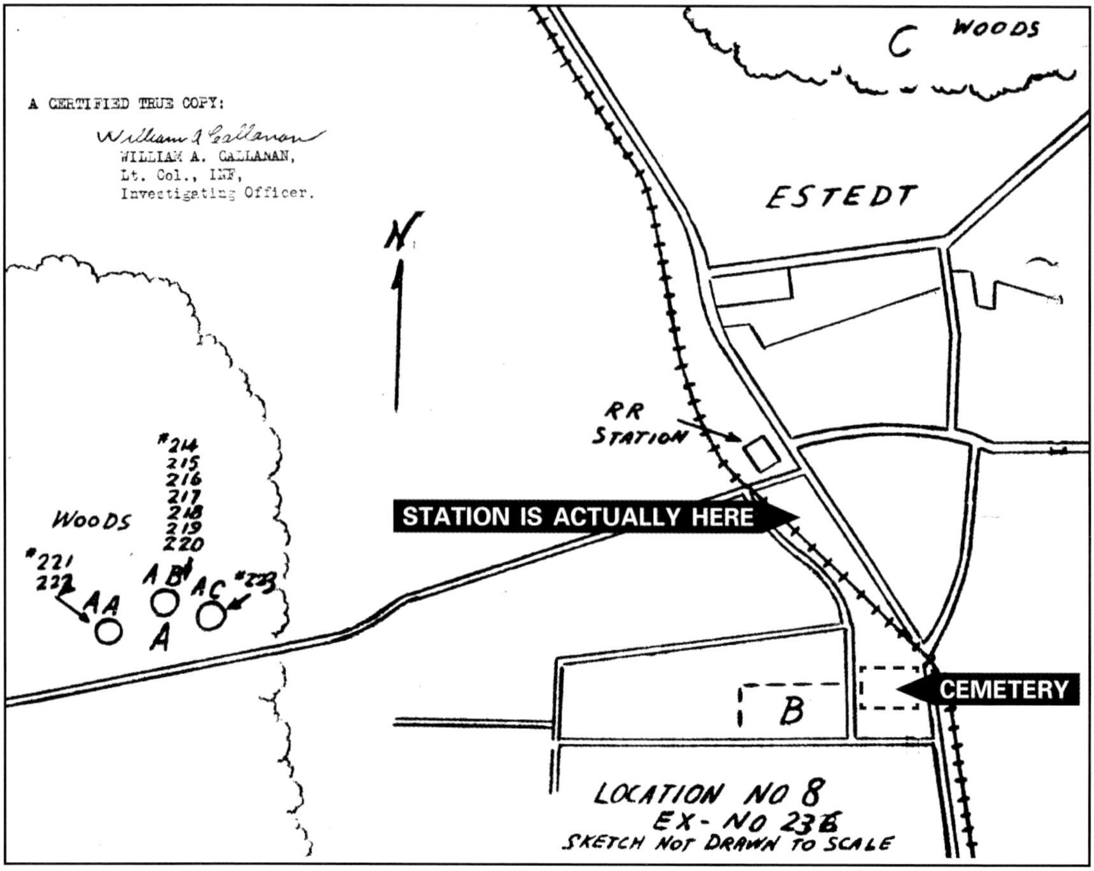

The second-largest mass murder in the Gardelegen area (after that at the barn) took place at the village of Estedt, seven kilometres north of Gardelegen, Here, on April 12, Fallschirmjäger soldiers executed 104 prisoners in a wood behind the village railway station, burying them in three large pits and two smaller ones. (NIOD)

horse-drawn carts requisitioned by burgomaster Krüger. The column was followed by a detail of 10-20 prisoners who had orders to bury anyone who died or was shot on the way.

The first group, which left around noon, initially marched east along the R188 main road towards Gardelegen. At Wernitz, only two kilometres further on, Fallschirmjäger lined up 25 of the weaker prisoners along the side of the road and killed them with machine pistols. At Solpke, about halfway to Gardelegen, the group began a wide detour to the north through the woods. When they reached an intersection in the forest, the guards allowed them to rest but about 15 prisoners who were too exhausted to go on were shot and buried on the spot. Passing through Breitenfeld, the remainder reached Zichtau at 2200, where they rested for an hour before turning south again following the R71 main road through Wiepke and Estedt to reach Gardelegen and the Remonte-Schule at about 0530 hours on the 12th.

The second group initially marched north-east along secondary roads through the woods towards Breitenfeld. Just after leaving Mieste, the column was strafed by Allied aircraft. Armed townspeople helped to round up the scattered prisoners. From Breitenfeld, the column cut due east and

A month later, German civilians recovered the remains of the victims under American supervision. This pit, [AA] on the sketch, contained 60 bodies. (NIOD)

The same spot in the woods today. (Karel Margry)

reached the village of Estedt where they turned north on to the R71 towards Wiepke. Shortly before dark, a German officer passing on a motorbike shouted to the guards that American tanks were coming towards them. The SS men quickly ordered the column to about face, beating them and firing their weapons to make them obey. Shortly after, the SS men fled. The prisoners, now free, stopped to camp for the night at Grauen Busch, a copse to the east of the main road between Wiepke and Schenkenhorst.

A few hours later, Fallschirmjäger troops took over the guarding of this dwindling group. (Gardelegen was the main depot of Germany's Fallschirmjäger troops, and there were many paratroop units stationed in the area. By 1945 they were mostly made up of redundant Luftwaffe personnel assigned to the Fallschirmjäger army.) Between April 11-13 these

The presence of the mass graves in the forest remained unknown to the Americans until May 9, 1945, when a freed Polish worker reported them to 1st Lieutenant Kenneth L. Russ, commander of 2nd Platoon, Battery D, 548th Anti-Aircraft Artillery & Automatic Weapons Battalion, which had been assigned Military Government duties at Estedt. Russ warned higher authorities and next day Lieutenant Colonel William A. Calannan, one of the officers investigating the Gardelegen war crimes, instructed him to have the bodies recovered and properly buried. Russ informed the burgomaster to have all the able-bodied men out on the morning of May 11 to carry out the task. This pit, [AB] on the sketch, contained 30 dead. (NIOD)

A GI watches while the corpses are put on the cart.
(NIOD)

Nothing remains to mark the massacre that took place here.
(Karel Margry)

Fallschirmjäger exercised a ruthless reign of terror, shooting most of the prisoners that came into their hands. One of the largest executions took place on the morning of the 12th at a locality known as Sandkuhle, in the woods just west of the Estedt railway station. On orders of NSDAP-Ortsgruppenleiter Fritz Korts, a group of six Fallschirmjäger commanded by Oberleutnant Helmut Hockhauf told local civilians to bring prisoners, both dead and live ones, thereto on horse-drawn carts. Six Polish forced labourers and three German civilians were ordered to dig two big trenches. The prisoners arrived in five cart-loads – three of 30-35 men each, one of ten, and one of four. The dead prisoners were thrown into the grave pits. Those still alive were made to kneel on the edge and killed by the paratroopers with a neck shot. The prisoners from the second cart had to cover those of the first with a layer of sand, before they too were shot and pushed into the same hole. One Pole kissed the shoes of one of the soldiers, begging not to shoot him, but he too was killed. The soldiers were enjoying themselves, callously joking and smoking cigarettes while

The 104 bodies recovered from the wood were buried in the Estedt village cemetery together with six more prisoners, murdered by the Fallschirmjäger, whose remains had been found in single graves in and around Estedt. (NIOD)

The same plot in Estedt cemetery today. The individual crosses have gone, and the large central cross has been moved to a corner of the plot. (The position of the cemetery [B] as given on the sketch on page 116 is not quite accurate, so we have added the correct position.) (Karel Margry)

A formal funeral ceremony was held on May 12, with Lieutenant Russ' platoon of the 548th AAA & AW Battalion furnishing the Guard of Honour. The wood visible on the horizon is where the mass murder had taken place. (NIOD)

they carried out the mass murder. A total of 104 dead were later recovered from this spot, plus another six from individual graves around the town.

That same afternoon, a group of some 120 prisoners who had become separated from the main column at Grauen Busch, and had spent the night without guards, was overtaken near Estedt by nine Fallschirmjäger in a car who again took them prisoner and led them into a wood (probably the same one where Oberleutnant Hockhauf's men had just shot the others). The prisoners were told to undress, and six of them were ordered to dig a trench. At the last moment, a messenger arrived in a car with an order from the Gardelegen chief of police that the prisoners were to be taken to the Remonte School at Gardelegen. The messenger was Hans-Joachim Korts, son of Ortsgruppenleiter Korts. After shooting those prisoners that had fainted on the spot, the Fallschirmjäger sent the men on their way, without escort, south to Gardelegen, where they arrived at the Remonte-Schule about 2200 hours on the 12th.

The remnants of the group camping at Grauen Busch, about 80-100 men, were transported to Gardelegen on horse-drawn wagons in the afternoon of the 13th. They too would become victims of the barn massacre.

By then, the third group from Mieste – the carts carrying the weak and the ill, with a column of marching prisoners in front – had long since arrived at Gardelegen. Guarded by only two SS men, it had followed the first group to Solpke. Here 23 of the prisoners were shot. The rest of the column stayed for the night in a farm barn at the village. Next morning, April 12, they made a small loop south across the railway to Solpke-Süd, recrossing it three kilometres further on at Weteritz before turning east onto the R188 main road again to reach the Remonte-Schule about 0500.

All along the various routes from Mieste, hastily-dug graves marked the places where prisoners had been shot or died from exhaustion: 33 at Wernitz, 23 at Solpke, 20 at Breitenfeld, 10 at Zichtau, 110 at Estedt, 8 at Berge.

The reaction of the German population to the sight of these columns of pitiable creatures passing their farms and villages showed the entire spectrum of human behaviour, varying from outright hatred . . . to total indifference . . . to compassion and help. Too often, citizens assisted the henchmen by denouncing prisoners for taking away a few beets or potatoes, by pointing out where escapees were hiding. Many who ventured to offer food or drink to the famished prisoners were chased off by guards. A handful risked their lives giving shelter to escapees. Farm milkman Karl Stegert from Weteritz helped three prisoners hiding in a hay loft, providing them with food and civilian clothes for three days until liberation. Vicar Friedrich Franz of Gardelegen and his wife hid four Dutch prisoners in their stable and cared for them until the arrival of the Americans.

Even as they entered Gardelegen, the men in their striped prison garments were not safe from persecution. Throughout the 12th and the 13th, murder squads from the SS and Fallschirmjäger soldiers on motorbikes roamed the streets, opening fire on prisoners straggling behind a column or spotted without escort. Four were shot in Bahnhofstrasse, two in front of the St Spiritus Hospital, two near the Salzwedeler Tor, and four on Rathausplatz. At least 12 persons were thus killed in the town. Their corpses were taken to the town cemetery and buried in common graves.

AT THE REMONTE SCHOOL

Thus, by the afternoon of Friday, April 13, a large number of camp prisoners – well over 1,000 – was assembled at the Remonte-Schule. The order to concentrate them in one place had been given by Gardelegen's acting burgomaster, Karl Lepa, on Tuesday the 10th after he saw the first groups of prisoners passing through his town. Initially they had been assembled at the Schützenhaus hall in the centre of town but when this became too crowded (and also because the citizens feared that the prisoners might make the hall dirty) they were transferred to the military barracks. The rumour quickly spread in the area that Gardelegen had been declared a hospital town and all prisoners there would be handed over to the Americans without a fight. This made even some prisoners who had already escaped come out of hiding and report in to Gardelegen voluntarily.

At the Remonte School the prisoners were put in two big stables and in the open-air riding ring. They received bread and soup, for many the first food since their evacuation from the camps began. The Remonte School commander, Oberstleutnant Hilmar Hubertus Freiherr von Seherr-Thoss, had left for Seethen on the 11th (he was taking most of the school horses there) leaving the Remonte-Schule in charge of Rittmeister Rudolf Kuhn, assisted by Seherr-Thoss's adjutant, Hauptmann Peter Freise.

Last stop before mass murder. The Remonte-Schule on Bismarker Strasse in Gardelegen, where the various groups of prisoners trekking through Kreis Gardelegen were assembled on April 10-13. A training establishment for cavalry horses, the Remount School had carried out its normal function until right before the prisoners arrived, most of the horses only having been evacuated on April 11. (Karel Margry)

To make up for the guards that had taken off, the SS convoy commanders again looked for new recruits among the prisoners, asking the ethnic Germans among them to volunteer. Twenty-five stepped forward, not just Germans but also a few Poles, a Czech, etc. Rittmeister Kuhn had them issued with German military uniforms.

Meanwhile, local Party and military leaders were conferring on what to do with the prisoners. To them, the situation was getting acute. The Americans were approaching rapidly and it was only a question of hours before they would reach Gardelegen and liberate the detainees. The Germans were well aware that the concentration camp inmates constituted damning evidence of the Nazis' criminal regime. In their minds, distorted by years of racial ideology, camp inmates were all criminals or 'sub-humans', who needed to be eliminated.

The driving force behind all this was the acting NSDAP-Kreisleiter (Nazi party district leader) of Gardelegen, 34-year-old Gerhard Thiele. In early April, Thiele had attended a meeting at Dessau called by Gauleiter Rudolf Jordan of Gau Magdeburg-Anhalt. On April 6, Thiele himself had called a meeting of the Ortsgruppenleiters and other officials of his Kreis at one of the Spilner restaurants in Gardelegen. Here, he issued an instruction 'on orders of the Gauleiter' that any prisoner who looted, tried to escape, offered resistance or was found wandering without proper papers was to

Kreisleiter Gerhard Thiele, the man chiefly responsible for the Gardelegen atrocity. Born in Stettin on April 29, 1909, Thiele joined the Nazi party in January 1931. He began work as a teacher in April but was fired in November because of his NSDAP membership. In 1932 he took command of the Deutsche Jungvolk (the predecessor of the Hitlerjugend) in the Finkenwalde district. Reinstated as a teacher after the Nazis came to power in 1933, he switched to the Hitlerjugend rising to become a Bannführer in 1937. That same year he became director of the Gebietsführerschule (School for Hitlerjugend Region Leaders) for the Mittelelbe region at Thale in the Harz. He was in the army in 1939-41 and 1942-43 serving in France and Russia and reaching the rank of Oberleutnant der Reserve, returning to the Hitlerjugend School at Thale in between. Recalled from the front as 'indispensable' in April 1943, he attended the NSDAP cadre school at Sonthofen and in May 1944 was appointed acting Kreisleiter of Gardelegen.
(Gedenkstätte Gardelegen)

be shot on the spot. Around this time, Thiele mentioned a subject he was to stress over and over again that week until the Volkssturm and many of the people of Gardelegen were well acquainted with it. He told of how the forced workers at Kakerbeck, a village 16 kilometres north of Gardelegen, had escaped before the Americans arrived, looted the homes and raped the women and children. He emphasized that he would not let that happen at Gardelegen. His attempts to alarm the people were successful in that, by the 13th, many believed that while killing the prisoners was horrible, it was necessary for the safety of the town.

Things came to a head with the arrival, and halt, of the two evacuation trains at Mieste on the 9th and Letzlingen on the 11th. On the 11th, Thiele for the first time voiced his intention to kill all the prisoners then being assembled at the Remonte-Schule. On the 12th, on receiving news of the mass escape at Letzlingen, he issued the order that escaped prisoners were to be hunted down and shot when caught.

During Wednesday the 11th, Thursday the 12th and Friday the 13th there were constant conferences – in person and by telephone – between Thiele and members of his Kreisleitung staff on the one hand; and Rittmeister Kuhn at the Remonte School; the SS convoy commanders Brauny, Locke and Rose, also at the Remonte barracks; the commanders of the two Volkssturm battalions in Kreis Gardelegen, Hans Debrodt and Rudolf Kampe; the Luftwaffe airfield commander, Oberst Walther Milz; and the Fallschirmjäger depot commander, Oberstleutnant Cord von Einem on the other hand. Few of them voiced any protest at Thiele's announcement that all prisoners were to be killed.

His first idea was to shoot them all in the grounds of the Remonte-Schule, but when he told Kuhn and Brauny this about 1730 on the 12th they objected to this because of the school's close proximity to the town. Thiele's next proposal was to kill them all at the Isenschnibber Scheune, the big barn of the Isenschnibbe farm estate which stood isolated on top of a small hill two kilometres north-east of the town. It was a big masonry barn with a tile roof, about 45 metres long, 18 metres wide and seven metres high, with four big double sliding doors, two in either long side. Used for storing the products of the harvest, it was now empty save for a knee-deep covering of straw on the floor.

At 2100, Thiele telephoned Rittmeister Kuhn at the Remonte-Schule and told him to inform Brauny that the prisoners were to be shot at the barn. Kuhn could not find Brauny so he passed the

The Isenschnibbe barn – site of the largest and most-horrific single mass murder of camp prisoners committed by the Nazi regime in the final weeks of the war. This is the southern facade of the building, pictured by US Army photographer Tech/5 Philip R. Mark on April 16, one day after the Americans discovered the atrocity. The 1,050 prisoners had been herded into the barn through the door on the left. The small shed on the left was where the Kapo guards who assisted the SS in the murder action stored the drum of petrol; some of them used it as a place to sleep during the night of the massacre. (USNA)

Today only a section of the southern wall of the barn has been preserved as a memorial. (Karel Margry)

order to the latter's elderly assistant, SS-Hauptscharführer Friedrich Teply, advising him to get the order confirmed in writing. Apparently, Brauny did not like the order and notified Volkssturm battalion commander Debrodt at the Kreisleitung of his reservations. When Thiele telephoned Debrodt from his home around midnight and heard of Brauny's unwillingness, he reacted angrily: 'If the convoy commander won't do it, hang him'.

Throughout the next day – Friday, April 13 – preparations for the massacre continued. At 1100 Debrodt, who was Thiele's most fanatical supporter, telephoned Kuhn at the Remonte-Schule and, on learning that the execution order had still not been carried out, cursed both Kuhn and Brauny for the failure. Brauny was still not available so Debrodt then spoke to Teply and apparently convinced him, for when the SS man laid down the receiver he said to Kuhn: 'It must be done'.

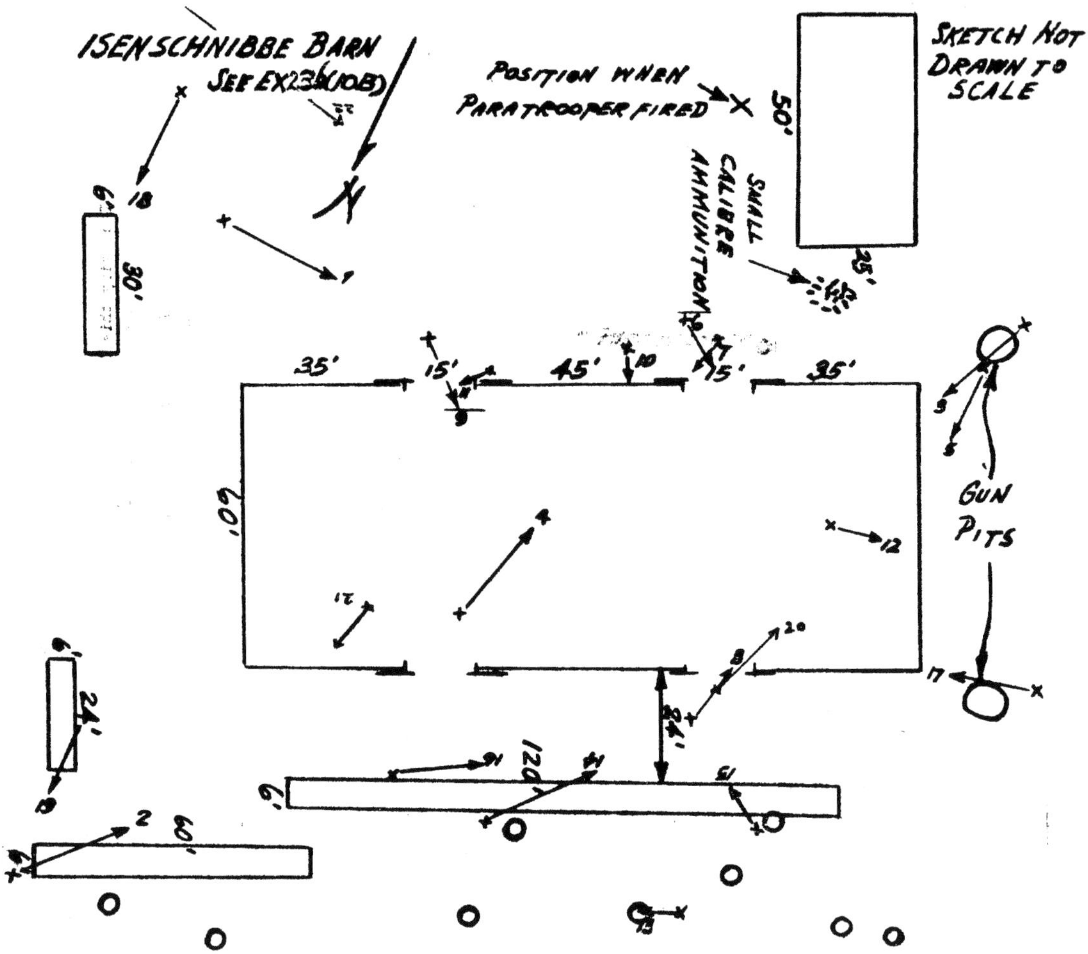

Sketch of the murder barn prepared by the US Army war crime investigators, showing the spot from where a Fallschirmjäger fired his machine pistol to make the prisoners move into the barn faster; the positions of the two machine guns that covered the doors; the spot near the small shed where a pile of spent ammunition was found; and the four ditches where the Germans buried about half of the victims on the morning after the massacre. The small circles indicate positions where dead prisoners were found who were killed escaping from the barn. The numbered arrows refer to pictures taken by the Signal Corps photographers as exhibits for the case file. Note that the sketch is drawn looking north to south. (NIOD)

Shortly after, Brauny asked the 25 newly-recruited Kapo guards which of them could handle a rifle. Seven said they could not, and they were told to step out of the group and stay in the barracks. The other 18 were issued with rifles and ammunition. Hauptmann Freise told them they were now free and would get food, schnapps and cigarettes if they would assist with shooting the other prisoners.

Debrodt called again at 1500 hours, urging Kuhn to take over command of the prisoners, but Kuhn declined saying he had nothing to do with them. About 1630, Walther Pannwitz, one of Debrodt's company commanders, telephoned Kuhn to ask for soldiers to guard and shoot the prisoners. Kuhn replied he had none. Pannwitz then tried Oberst Milz at the airfield, but he too said he had no one available for this task.

MASS MURDER AT THE ISENSCHNIBBE BARN

About 1600, the guards at the Remonte-Schule formed up some 1,050 prisoners in groups of 100 and columns of five. Then, in the late afternoon, they marched them out of the gate and up the road to the north in three large groups of about 300. Those too weak to march – about 100 – followed in three carts and trailers drawn by horses and tractors. Somehow, the Germans had assembled some 80 guards: 30 SS men, some of them with dogs; the 18 Kapo guards; half a dozen members of the Volkssturm and of the Reichsarbeitsdienst (Reich Labour Service); and 30 Luftwaffe soldiers from the nearby airfield. The march column was commanded by SS-Hauptscharführer Teply; Transportführer Brauny did not go to the barn (he disappeared from the Remonte-Schule sometime during the 13th); what his colleagues Rose and Locke did is unclear.

None of the prisoners had any inkling of the fate that awaited them. Rumours had it that they were being marched out to be handed over to the Americans. Guards told some of them that they were going to spend the night in a barn because of lack of space in the barracks.

It was less than two kilometres to the barn. When halfway, the column stopped on the road for about an hour. A tractor passed by with several cans of petrol and a case of ammunition. From afar, prisoners saw some of the load being carried inside the barn.

The last group of 300 arrived at the barn around 1900 hours. It was still daylight. Here, the 80 guards were joined by some 20 Fallschirmjäger, two of them on motorcycles, who arrived carrying Panzerfausts, machine pistols, hand-grenades and flare pistols. The prisoners on foot waited outside the barn for the carts with the sick to arrive, who were put inside first. An Allied aircraft was at that moment circling overhead, so when Unterscharführer Braun (one of the Ilfeld NCOs) ordered the others to move inside as well, many thought it was because of this. As the guards herded them in, a Fallschirmjäger soldier fired his machine pistol into the group to make them move faster, wounding one man. All entered through the south-west door. It was now 2000 hours.

Once inside, many immediately noticed the strong smell of petrol, but contented themselves with the thought that the barn must have been used as a garage or to store fuel. The prisoners were ordered to sit down. The four big doors were closed and wedged fast on the outside with stones.

A few minutes later, the door on the south-west side opened and two soldiers entered. One of them – identified as Braun by some – set fire to the straw with a match at several places. As soon as they had gone out, the prisoners rushed up and frantically put out the flames with their blankets, clothes and bare hands. Then they pushed all the straw to the middle of the barn. The soldiers re-entered and again ignited the floor by discharging the signal flares into the straw. Several times, the prisoners managed to put the fires out but finally the soldiers prevented them by throwing hand-

Left: **Bullet-riddled bodies of prisoners piled up against the south-east door. This is where three prisoners – Geza Bondi, Aurel Szobel and Stanislaw Waleszynski – escaped by digging a hole underneath the door. The man on the left tried to crawl out too, but he was shot at close range by one of the guards standing outside – as evidenced by the bullet hole in his right temple. The wooden doors, locked throughout the killing action, were only opened by the Volkssturm the next morning.** (NIOD)

The south-east door is the only one left standing today. Careful comparison of the stonework confirms the location. (Karel Margry)

grenades, shooting Panzerfausts, and firing machine pistols and rifles into the frantic masses through the south-west door. The men inside reeled back. Others rushed sideways, pressing themselves against the barn wall to find protection against the bullets. A group of some 50 or 60 Russians rushed to the opposite side of the building. The north-west door was broken open and the prisoners started to run out. The Fallschirmjäger mowed them down with machine pistols and rifles. Two machine guns had been placed at the west side of the barn, one covering the northern and one the southern doors. Several of the armed prisoners – notably Kazimierz Drygalski, a Pole, and Adolf August Pinnenkämper, a German – joined in the killing, as did the crew of a nearby Flak battery, Hitlerjugend teenagers led by Wachtmeister Georg Bensch, who came running up with machine pistols.

Soon dead and dying men were piling up at all the doors. Cries of pain and panic rung inside the dark building, as others were trampled. To escape the rain of bullets, some men feigned death or hid under the dead bodies of others. By now the fire was completely out of control. The inside of the barn began to fill up with a suffocating smoke. Chaos and panic was complete. Men were swearing, crying, pleading, praying, shouting 'Vive la France!' and 'Long live Poland!' – several even broke out singing their national anthem. Men were being roasted alive. Human torches ran around until they dropped to the ground dead. Others suffocated or were killed by the exploding hand-grenades and Panzerfausts.

Unbelievably, some men managed to survive this holocaust. Mieczeslaw

The north side of the barn, where the doors were rammed by the Russian prisoners. The sliding doors were blocked on the outside with stones, but pressure from the men inside caused them to hinge upwards. This created openings left and right through which prisoners ran out, only to be met by a rain of bullets. As far as is known, only three men escaped alive on this side: Mieczeslaw Kolodziejski and Fedor Dugin through the north-east door after dark, and Stanislaw Majewicz through the north-west one pictured here, after it had been blown open by an exploding hand-grenade. In the foreground is one of the trenches dug by the Volkssturm to bury the victims. (USNA)

Behind the memorial wall a low wall now delineates the contours of the barn. (Karel Margry)

A close-up of the north-west door, with burned, half-burned and trampled bodies piled up in a heap. One can picture the horror: as one man fell hit, his comrade who followed stumbled and fell over him, those coming behind adding to the heap until it formed a wall of bodies which then further trapped those inside. A few prisoners owed their life to it, using it as shelter against the bullets and flames. Note the bullet marks on the wall. Looking across the inside of the barn, one can also see the hole in the west wall caused by a Panzerfaust being fired right through it. (USNA)

Kolodziejski, a Pole, was in the barn with his father. They were among those who tried to get out through the north-west door, which the Russians were trying to push open. The father was killed there, but the son got out. However, when he saw a German shooting the men outside with a pistol, he scurried back into the barn. Every time he or others approached the door, the Germans fired. Finally, he went to the north-east door and managed to crawl out there after dark, escaping to the woods in the south-east.

Fedor Dugin, a Russian, also got out through this same north-east door and he too hid in the woods.

By then, the north-west door had been blown open by the exploding hand-grenades. Stanislaw Majewicz, a Pole, escaped through here. His friend Zdzislaw Klipacki, who was running a few metres behind him, was caught by SS men and shot. Majewicz dropped to the ground and lay still, pretending to be dead. Later he managed to creep away.

The south-west door. Despite the hail of bullets fired at it, five men – Wlodzimierz Wozny, Romuald Bak, Witold Modzelewski, Dimitri Pietrov and Amaro Castellvi – managed to escape through here. The corpses lying in the foreground may be in the position where they were shot trying to escape, but more likely they were pulled out of the barn by the Volkssturm when these laboured to cover up the crime afterwards. The man lying on the left has lost a foot, no doubt blown off by one of the hand-grenades thrown into the barn. (USNA)

Another Pole, Wlodzimierz Wozny, dug a hole near the south-west door to get fresh air. He tried to get out, was shot at and ran back. A hand-grenade wounded him above the left hip and in the back. After dark, he tried again. Flat on his belly, he worked his way out, keeping close to the barn wall. Leaping up suddenly, he tried to barge his way through the string of guards. A dog grabbed him. Guards came running, beating him up and firing their rifles, but Wozny shouted in German to stop shooting. The brief confusion allowed him to escape in the dark. He hid in a barn.

Another Pole, Romuald Bak, took advantage of the consternation caused by Wozny's action to make good his own escape. Lying close to where the latter made his bid for freedom, and with the guards in front of him vacating their post to grab Wozny, Bak saw a gap appear in the cordon and, rolling his body on the ground, managed to get through unnoticed.

At least three more men – Witold Modzelewski, a Pole; Dimitri Pietrov, a Russian; and Amaro Castellvi, a Frenchman – crawled out over the bodies through this south-west door, then made for the woods to the east.

The interior of the barn, looking down the long axis toward the west wall. This picture, taken by war photographer William Vandivert of *LIFE* magazine, clearly shows the roof support posts up which Armand Dureux and others climbed to escape the flames and bullets. Note the hole in the far left corner caused by the Panzerfausts. Many of the bodies had already been taken out of the barn when this picture was taken. (Gedenkstätte Gardelegen)

Looking down the empty shell of the roofless barn today. (Karel Margry)

A scene from Dante's Hell. One of the victims still in the position where he collapsed from smoke inhalation after the Germans set fire to the straw on the floor. Picture taken by Sergeant E. R. Allen of the 168th Signal Photo Company on April 16 and approved for release by SHAEF on the 19th. (USNA)

Three prisoners – Geza Bondi and Aurel Szobel from Hungary and an unnamed Pole – escaped by digging a hole underneath the south-east door. Scraping away at the door's concrete foundation with a table-spoon and bare hands, they found it consisted only of a thin layer. The stones underneath could be removed by hand. They clawed for an hour before they had an opening big enough. By then it was getting dark so they hoped they could get away unseen. The first to go out was the unnamed Pole. Just as he reached the corner of the building, a guard dog came sniffling by. The Pole tried to simulate death, but the beast howled and a guard came running and shot the man. Szobel and Bondi waited until the dog and its master had gone to the other side of the building before crawling out and away through the grain fields, finding refuge in a damaged building near the airfield.

Possibly, the unnamed Pole was Stanislaw Waleszynski; if so, he was not killed. Waleszynski scraped a hole with a table-spoon together with two others (whom he remembered as another Pole and a Frenchman) also underneath the south-east door. All three went through, crawling on their belly to the south-east corner. Waleszynski heard a dog barking, and some Germans shout 'Don't shoot!' at the other end of the barn. (This was again the consternation caused by Wozny's break-out.) With the guards and dogs thus distracted, Waleszynski struck east for the woods.

Boris Mamajow, a Russian, crawled out this same south-east door with another Russian after dark. A German came along with a dog and a flashlight but they were not discovered. After crawling 300 metres, they got up and made for the woods, but here they were discovered by German soldiers who threw hand-grenades at them. Mamajow's comrade was killed and he himself wounded in face and back. He crawled on through the woods for another two kilometres finding a hiding place in a bomb-damaged building.

Yet another Russian, Ivan Matwego, escaped through this south-east door after dark. He was spotted by one of the Kapo guards, Ludwig Juchocki, who hit him with his rifle and told him to go back in the barn. Matwego ran away and, laying himself down, feigned death. As he lay there, he saw Juchocki shoot three other prisoners. Later, he was able to get away.

Several men climbed up one of the barn's wooden support posts to escape the flames, bullets and explosions below. After ascending with a friend, Frenchman Armand Dureux urinated on his woollen cap and held it over his nose against the smoke. He could breathe better air through a hole in the roof. His friend was hit by a bullet and fell down, so he dropped down too to comfort him in his last minutes. After dark, he rushed out through the north-east door. Though struck by a bullet behind the ear, he managed to crawl away unseen, and hide in a barn two kilometres away.

Edward Antoniak, a Pole, held on to a roof beam, but after a few hours, half-fainted from the smoke, fell down too. Shrapnel wounded him in the head. Clambering over masses of charred corpses he made his way to the north-east door. A guard fired at him, so he dropped down, feigning death. After midnight, he sneaked out and escaped.

These men who got away all stayed in hiding until the arrival of the

None of the prisoners locked in the barn stood any great chance of survival, but those who stood absolutely no chance at all were the sick, weak and elderly. Numbering about 100, they were brought to the site on horse-cart and trailer and were carried into the barn and put in a corner. Unable to get up or move away from the flames, they burned to death where they lay. Coming two days after the discovery of Nordhausen, and on the same day as the liberation of Bergen-Belsen, Gardelegen received the same massive publicity given to these horror camps, its gruesome images shocking the free world and damning the Nazi regime. (IWM)

Despite the horrible effects of burning, this victim could still be recognised as being a black person. The US investigators at first assumed that he might be the only American citizen imprisoned at 'Dora'. Surviving camp inmates interviewed by them spoke of a black prisoner they had met at Rottleberode camp and later at the Remonte-Schule who had claimed to be an American airman shot down over Magdeburg. He spoke English and had the letter 'A' sewn on the left side of his prison coat and on his right trouser leg. At Rottleberode he had worked as a camp doctor. However, some prisoners who themselves spoke English and had talked to the man, found his mastery of the language only fair and guessed he was French-African rather than American. Later investigation revealed that the American who had been a prisoner at 'Dora' had still been alive two weeks after the Gardelegen atrocity. Recent research has shown that the dead man was in fact Albert Wittenberg, a 35-year-old Dutch resistance fighter, originating from Suriname and arrested in Amsterdam in June 1944, who most likely came to Gardelegen from Hannover-Stöcken. This is one of a series of pictures taken by Pfc Larry R. Darcy of the 168th Signal Photo Company on April 19 under the specific direction of Lieutenant Colonel Edward E. Cruise, the chief investigating officer of the Gardelegen war crime case. (NIOD)

Americans. Others managed to remain alive in the burning smoke-filled barn. Herman Pranden, a German prisoner, dug a hole in the ground and lay down in it. He fainted during the night, but did not die.

Mieczyslaw Lawnicek, a Pole, crawled up against a pile of dead near the door to find protection against the smoke and flames. Other men who did the same pushed him further and further away until he lay virtually outside the barn. There he remained, just a few metres away from the armed cordon, pretending to be one of the dead. A guard shot at one of the wounded on the pile and this man's blood and brains splattered all over Lawnicek's face. He kept motionless, remaining in this position all night.

Georges Crétin, a Frenchman, crawled to one of the doors to breathe. He saw two of his comrades, Jean Desvignes and Jean Paris, be killed by the bullets trying to get out. Hit in his left thigh, he was buried under the bodies of other men while the deadly flames crept near. Despite a rain of bullets fired at him from the outside, he managed to free himself, taking cover behind a pile of dead. Hours later, withdrawing deeper inside the barn, Crétin lay down among the smouldering corpses and fell asleep.

One of his compatriots, Guy Chamaillard, took shelter under the bodies of men hit. As more men were killed, the pile of corpses grew to a height of five feet. Covered in blood but unhurt, Chamaillard stayed in this position all night without losing consciousness. Later, he too moved away from the door and went to sleep among the corpses.

Eugenius Siradzki, a Pole, kept alive by keeping his mouth to a small hole in the wall near the ground for air, and covering his body with blankets. He

Geza Bondi, one of the handful of men who survived the massacre, shows US soldiers how he managed to escape, digging a hole underneath the south-east door and crawling away after dark. Bondi, a 37-year-old bank employee and musician from Budapest, Hungary, and a former 1st Lieutenant in the Hungarian Army, had been arrested on November 12, 1944. He was first imprisoned at Flossenbürg concentration camp, later moved to 'Dora', and then to Ilfeld, being put to work making fuel pumps for aircraft. He was in the train to Mieste, and arrived at the Remonte-Schule early on the 12th. After escaping from the barn, he hid for two days, reporting in to the Americans on the 15th. (USNA)

fainted, but did not suffocate. He too was completely covered with bodies which protected him against the flames.

Yevgeni Kateba, a Russian, was thrown to the north end of the barn by an exploding hand-grenade and covered by about ten corpses of men killed by the explosions. Unable to move, he remained in this position all night.

Two more Russians – Leonid Maistrov (who had his clothes blown off him by the explosions) and Wasel Momochuk – managed to stay alive, sheltering under the piles of cooling, then calcifying, stinking bodies. The exact total number of prisoners who survived the massacre has never been established but appears to be around 25.

The murder action continued well into the night, with German troops and Kapo guards watching the doors and walls for any escape attempts. In all, some 50 hand-grenades were thrown into the barn. Around 2100 hours, the Fallschirmjäger went back to their depot to get a new supply of ammunition and Panzerfausts. They fired the Panzerfausts into the barn through the west wall and the south-west door. About midnight, the paratroopers received an alert and left.

Shortly after, Kreisleiter Thiele, who had been present from about 2200 (he had been conferring with Oberst Milz at the airfield before that), returned to the Remonte-Schule with Unterscharführer Braun and ordered four of the Kapo guards left there (from the seven who had said they could not shoot) to collect a drum of petrol at the Kreisleitung garage and bring it to the barn so as to complete the incineration of the bodies. Once there, the men were told to stay on as guards.

The important thing for the Nazis now was to eradicate any sign of the atrocity that had taken place before the arrival of the Americans. From midnight until about 0230 Thiele and Debrodt were on the phone at the Kreisleitung headquarters, mobilising local organisations to help with burying the dead and clearing up the site.

The first to arrive, at 0430 on April 14, were 50 Volkssturm men from the neighbouring village of Kloster Neuendorf, joined later in the morning by 15 men of the Gardelegen fire brigade, 15 from the Technische Nothilfe (technical emergency service), and 90 from the Gardelegen Volkssturm. In all, some 170 persons were at hand. Few of them had been told beforehand what to expect.

The SS men and armed Kapos were still at the barn doing their dirty work. Thiele, having returned there, ordered all survivors to be shot. Opening the doors and entering the still-smoking building, the SS men and Kapos called out that they were ready to give out medical aid to anyone who was still alive. However, this was a trick, as survivors who made their presence known were killed on the spot with a bullet through the head. This went on until 0830 when the last of the SS men and Kapos returned to Gardelegen.

Meanwhile, the Volkssturm men had begun to dig four grave trenches, two metres wide and two metres deep – two long ones on the north side of the barn and two smaller ones on the east side. Many of the bodies were

Two Polish survivors tell their stories to Allied war correspondents. Wlodzimierz Wozny (centre), a 21-year-old medical student from Lvov, was arrested in November 1942 for issuing medical unfitness slips to Polish POWs being sent to Germany. He was imprisoned at Lublin, Buchenwald, Flossenbürg, 'Dora', and finally Wieda, being evacuated with the train to Letzlingen. He escaped through the south-west door by barging his way through a cluster of German guards. Eugenius Siradzki (right), 33, a painter from Sosnowiec, was arrested there in November 1944 for black market activities. He was imprisoned at Myslowice concentration camp before being sent to Gross-Rosen, then 'Dora', then Rottleberode. He remained inside the barn throughout the massacre night and the subsequent cleaning operation by the Volkssturm, not leaving the scene until the morning of the 15th. The GI on the left translating for the Poles could be either Tech/4 Henryk Postrosny of the 327th Engineer Combat Battalion, 102nd Division, or Pfc Emil J. Schirl of the 113th Evacuation Hospital, both of whom acted as sworn-in interpreters for the Poles interviewed by the American war crimes investigators. (IWM)

totally charred, and the workers used hooks and pronged forks to pull individual corpses from the smoking piles of dead. As they worked to empty the building the men found prisoners who had survived the carnage. Some of them were so horribly wounded that they begged to be shot. Hermann Hohls, the Volksturm company commander in charge of the work; Gustav Palis, one of his men; and Paul Schernikau, the fire brigade chief, each shot a prisoner to put him out of his misery.

Some of the workers objected to the horrible task and could not stand the shooting and the cries and moans of the wounded. A few of them left the scene in defiance of orders. Schernikau refused Thiele's order to sprinkle the petrol over the corpses, and left at 1000 taking the drum with him. Hohls sent a runner back to the Remonte-Schule to say that the Volkssturm men were unable to shoot the surviving prisoners. The runner came back with an Unteroffizier and five other soldiers. The Unteroffizier shot five prisoners in a most cold-blooded manner. A Russian prisoner who came walking out of the barn naked was grabbed, forced to kneel on the edge of one of the trenches, and killed with a neck shot. Among the piles of dead, the few survivors not yet found – Crétin, Chamaillard, Lawnicek, Siradzki, Kateba, Maistrov, and a handful of others – kept deadly still, knowing that the slightest motion would betray them.

It must be said that not all those that came out of the barn were executed. When two workers grabbed his foot with a hayrack, Wasel Momochuk turned around and said: 'I am not dead'. The Volkssturm men ran away scared and Momochuk followed them out. Though wounded, he was allowed to sit in the sun. Herman Pranden, when he came to, walked out too. They and two other survivors were not harmed but given sandwiches, then put on the fire brigade truck and taken to Jävenitz where they joined the other prisoners that were assembled there.

Only about half of the victims had been buried when, at 1730, the work was broken off because of the approach of American forces.

THE AMERICANS DISCOVER THE MASSACRE SITE

Around 1700 hours on April 14, the US 102nd Infantry Division reached the town of Gardelegen. The division was advancing eastward from Hannover to Stendal as part of US Ninth Army's grand sweep towards the Elbe. The 2nd Battalion of the 405th Regiment approached the town from the north. After negotiations with the town commander, Oberst Milz, who would only surrender to a full colonel, the German garrison formally capitulated at 1900 hours. Some 500 troops were taken prisoner.

Meanwhile, Chamaillard and the other survivors still languished in the barn. Too weak, too wounded or too dazed to move away from it, they had stayed inside. Three of them – Siradzki, Kateba and Maistrov – hid on the rafters in case the Germans returned. Later they climbed down, warming themselves beside the still-burning corpses, only going to the door to see if anybody was coming. Another night fell. The following morning, April 15, three escaped Russian prisoners of war found the barn. From them, those inside learned of the arrival of the Americans the evening before. Searching the barn, they found Crétin who until then had lain undiscovered among the corpses. The Russians helped the survivors reach the Luftwaffe barracks on the nearby airfield, now in American hands. Here they were given food and medical treatment. A few hours later, the patrol from the 2nd Battalion stumbled on the Isenschnibbe barn by accident, uncovering the atrocity.

The Americans were shocked by the ghastly crime and made sure that it was immediately made known to the world. Over the next few days, dozens of Allied war correspondents, cameramen and photographers visited the barn to report on the atrocity and document the gruesome sight. Numerous American units sent truckloads of GIs to Gardelegen to let them see for themselves the crimes committed by the Nazi regime they were fighting. They explored the barn with wet handkerchiefs pressed to their faces to overcome the awful stench.

The commander of the 102nd Division, Major General Frank A. Keating, ordered that the burgomasters and prominent citizens of Gardelegen and all neighbouring villages be conducted to the barn to see the horrible sight. On April 18, under supervision of divisional troops, the German dignitaries viewed the still-smouldering victims of the mass murder, and were formally charged with telling their communities the sordid tale.

General Keating also directed that every available male citizen of Gardelegen be required to help disinter the victims and give them a proper burial. On the morning of April 18, some 250-300 men assembled on the market square with shovels, spades, bedsheets and pieces of rope. Formed up in columns of five, and escorted by GI guards and Sherman tanks, the civilians were marched to the barn. There, while men of the 327th Engineer Combat Battalion stood by with fixed

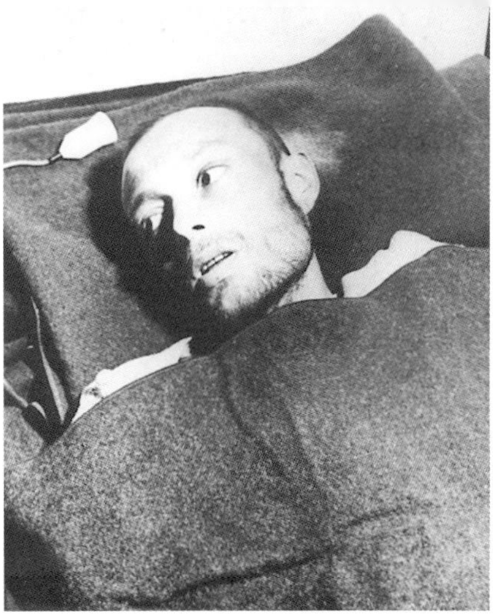

One of the four known French survivors. Georges Crétin from St Claude was rounded up in February 1943 in a reprisal raid after the killing of a German officer. He was seriously wounded in his left thigh as he tried to break out of the barn, but survived under a pile of bodies. Lying among the hundreds of dead in the centre of the barn, he was not discovered by the other survivors until two days later. He was pictured at the hospital on Gardelegen airfield while recovering from his wounds and the effects of starvation. (IWM)

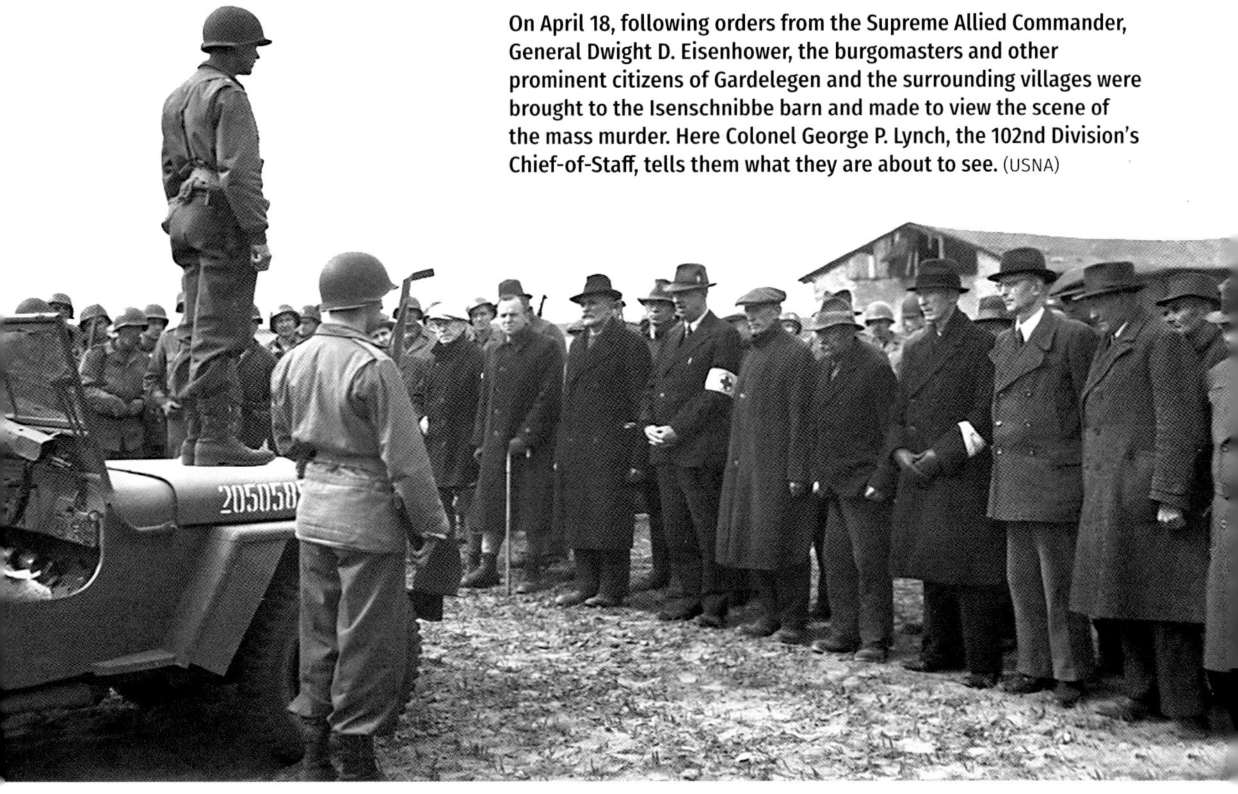

On April 18, following orders from the Supreme Allied Commander, General Dwight D. Eisenhower, the burgomasters and other prominent citizens of Gardelegen and the surrounding villages were brought to the Isenschnibbe barn and made to view the scene of the mass murder. Here Colonel George P. Lynch, the 102nd Division's Chief-of-Staff, tells them what they are about to see. (USNA)

Watched by grim-looking GIs, Colonel Lynch (in foreground) shows the Germans the burial trench near the north-west door, already filling up with ground water. (USNA)

MP
MP

Three of the Germans view the body of a victim inside the barn. (USNA)

bayonets, they dug up the dead from the thinly-covered mass graves and carried out the bodies that were still in the barn.

The American guards were in a foul mood and used rifle butts to drive unwilling workers into the barn. The Germans had to move the dead with bare hands and no one was allowed to wear gloves. At one point, there was even a fake execution, a large group of Germans being put against the barn wall and a firing-squad of GIs taking aim. Freed camp inmates were brought to the site to point out men they knew to be implicated. The Americans had trouble preventing the former prisoners from lynching those Nazis that were recognised. Freed Polish forced labourers and Russian prisoners of war beat and kicked the Germans and called out to the GIs to kill them all.

The Americans initially decided to bury the victims in common graves and accordingly the German workers began digging seven long trenches just south of the barn on the 18th. However, after two days, the 102nd Division received the order issued by the Supreme Allied Commander, General Dwight D. Eisenhower, that victims of Nazi atrocities were to be buried in individual graves. So work on the trenches was halted and those victims who had already been buried in them dug up again.

A final resting place was laid out according to the regulations for US military cemeteries about 150 metres south-west of the barn. Lieutenant

Between April 18-24, all able-bodied men of Gardelegen were compelled to help remove the corpses from the barn and burial trenches and re-inter them. The citizens were ordered to assemble on Rathausplatz with spades and shovels. This picture by Tech/5 Josef E. von Stroheim of the 168th Signal Photo Company was taken on April 22 when each man was also given a white cross to carry. (USNA)

The Deutsches Haus on Rathausplatz is still an inn today. (Karel Margry)

Ready to march off to the Isenschnibbe barn. (USNA)

Rathausplatz today, with the Rathaus (Town Hall) on the right. (Karel Margry)

Colonel William R. Douglas, CO of the 102nd Quartermaster Company, and 1st Lieutenant George A. Carlson of 1st Platoon, 3046th Graves Registration Company, supervised its construction which began on the 21st. The citizens of Gardelegen dug the graves, interred the bodies, erected either a cross or Star of David over each, and surrounded the entire site with a white fence.

On April 22, each man assembled in the town square was in addition given a white wooden cross to carry. The exhumation and burial took until

The column of citizen workers march down the Stendaler Strasse, escorted by a Sherman tank of the 701st Tank Battalion, 102nd Division. The Isenschnibbe barn is up the road on the left, then named the Alte Heerstrasse. (USNA)

The Alte Heerstrasse (Old Army Road) was renamed Strasse der Opfer des Faschismus (Road of the Victims of Fascism) in GDR times. Today one can no longer get to the barn via this route, the old road having been cut by the new B71 bypass road around Gardelegen which was opened in December 2000. However, one can still reach it via the other old route, Bismarker Strasse, a new viaduct having been built to carry it over the bypass, and also direct from the B71. (Karel Margry)

Watched by GIs of the 327th Engineer Combat battalion, the civilians remove the bodies from the long trench on the north side of the barn. Another picture from the series taken by Pfc Darcy under Lieutenant Colonel Cruise's direction on the 19th. (NIOD)

the 24th. A total of 574 corpses were recovered from the grave pits and 442 from the barn – adding up to a total of 1,016 victims. Of these, only four could be identified by name, another 301 merely by their prisoner number. The unidentified totalled 711. Nationality could be established of only 186 bodies: among the dead were 60 Poles, 52 Russians, 27 Frenchmen, 17 Hungarians, eight Belgians, five Germans, five Italians, four Czechs, four Yugoslavs, two Dutchmen, one Mexican and one Spaniard. A number of them were Jews. (After the war, a few more victims were identified from the recorded prisoner numbers.)

At the entrance to the cemetery, a big sign was erected with a text in English and German: 'Here lie 1,016 Allied prisoners of war who were murdered by their captors. They were buried by the citizens of Gardelegen,

The Americans purposely instructed that the citizens in white-collar suits were to carry the corpses – with their bare hands – assigning the task of digging to the others. Ironically, the workers included many who, only a week earlier, as members of the Volkssturm, had dug these same trenches and thrown bodies in them in the last-minute attempt to erase all traces of the atrocity. (NIOD)

who are charged with the responsibility that these graves are forever kept as green as the memory of these unfortunates will be kept in the hearts of freedom-loving men everywhere.'

General Keating ordered that the entire population attend a formal funeral ceremony which was held on the afternoon of April 25. Local families were impressed with the responsibility of forever caring for the graves of these victims of the Nazi regime, each being assigned one grave. To ensure that these instructions would be followed in later years, records were left with the city officials. The divisional Chief-of-Staff, Colonel George P. Lynch, communicated the feelings of his soldiers when he told the townspeople: 'You have lost the respect of the civilised world'.

After recovery, the bodies were laid out for identification. These ones lie between the two pits to the north-west of the barn – see the sketch on page 126. Picture taken by Pfc Darcy on the 19th. (NIOD)

Two GIs stand silent watch at corpses removed from the smaller pit on the east side of the barn. (NIOD)

Disinterred victims await reburial. In the background the civilians are filling in the emptied long trench to the north of the barn. (USNA)

Bodies taken from this same trench are laid out along the barn's western wall. (NIOD)

The 102nd Division initially decided to bury the victims in mass graves, ordering the Germans to dig seven parallel trenches just to the south of the barn. This picture is looking east, towards the Luftwaffe airfield which begins immediately beyond the dirt road in the background. (IWM)

Looking from the memorial grounds to the former airfield. (Karel Margry)

Freed prisoners were asked if they could identify victims and also to pick out implicated Germans from among the conscripted workers. Here, a Pole cries out for justice beside the body of a comrade. (IWM)

On the 20th a general instruction from SHAEF stipulated that victims of Nazi atrocities were to be buried in individual graves, so work on the mass graves was halted and the civilians were put to work constructing a proper cemetery. Laid out according to the rules for US military cemeteries, the cemetery had four large square plots separated by two crossing lanes. The total number of victims buried in the cemetery was 1,018 – the 1,016 murdered at the barn plus two escaped prisoners from the Letzlingen train who had been caught and executed by members of the Kloster Neuendorf Volkssturm at the Lindenthal forest lodge, just south-west of the town, on April 13. In this picture taken on the 22nd the cemetery is taking shape. While the first rows of graves have already been closed on the left, others are still being worked on. SHAEF had ruled that each victim was to be individually buried by a specified German, whose name was registered at the town hall and whose family was required to maintain that grave in perpetuity. Should the family die out or move away, the burgomaster was responsible for appointing a new caretaker for the grave. This picture by Tech/5 Mark also clearly illustrates how close the Isenschnibbe barn was to Gardelegen town which can be seen in the distance. The Remonte-Schule, where the prisoners were assembled before the massacre, is the tall building standing out between the two spires on the right. The doomed prisoners came marching up the hill to the barn along the tree-lined road on the left. (USNA)

The trees and bushes which have grown up around the cemetery obscure the view today.
(Karel Margry)

On Wednesday April 25, the entire population of Gardelegen was ordered to attend the formal dedication of the new cemetery. In 1945, the town had a population of 13,000. (USNA)

Colonel George E. Simmons, Protestant chaplain of the 102nd Division, speaks to the assembly at the funeral service. The roof of the murder barn can just be seen on the right above the audience. (USNA)

Taps is sounded, while the Guard of Honour stands by to fire another rifle volley.

AFTERMATH

The Americans immediately started a thorough investigation of the war crime. On April 17, Lieutenant Colonel Edward B. Beale, the Judge Advocate of the 102nd Division, made a preliminary inspection of the murder barn and interviewed a number of freed prisoners at Gardelegen. Between April 19 and May 22, Lieutenant Colonels Edward E. Cruise and William A. Callanan and Captain Samuel G. Weiss, investigating officers of the Ninth Army War Crimes Branch, collected sworn statements from 99 survivors, implicated Germans, and other eyewitnesses. Among those arrested by the Americans were Brauny (discovered in a POW camp) and one SS guard; Debrodt, Hohls, Pannwitz and six other Volkssturm members; Rittmeister Kuhn; Oberstleutnant von Einem; four members of Thiele's Kreisleitung staff; burgomaster Krüger of Mieste; and ten of the Kapo guards. The Germans and Kapos suspected of having actually killed someone were confined at Ninth Army Detention Camp No. 92 at Ziegenhain. Several of the implicated Germans committed suicide before they could be arrested, among them Volkssturm company commander Waldemar Schumm and one of Gardelegen's three Ortsgruppenleiters, Otto Palis.

On July 1, 1945, in accordance with inter-Allied agreements, the US Army handed over the province of Sachsen-Anhalt, which included Gardelegen, to the Soviet Military Administration. As the scene of crime was now in Soviet hands, it was now up to the Soviets to pursue the matter. A year later, on July 25, 1946, the Americans turned 21 of the implicated men over to the Russian authorities, together with a copy volume of all their documentation on the case, and on August 6, the US Army formally closed their own file. The Soviets sentenced most of the 21 to long years of incarceration or assigned them to long internment in one of their 'special camps' in Germany.

One man was not handed over to the Russians. Erhard Brauny was tried at the Nordhausen War Crime Trial which was held before the US Military Court at Dachau in 1947. He was sentenced to life, probably only escaping a death sentence because he convinced the judges that he had not been present at the barn when the murder action took place. He died from cancer in Landsberg prison on June 16, 1950. Brauny's assistant, Friedrich Teply, was a witness at Brauny's trial but he was never tried for his own part in the massacre. None of the other implicated SS commanders – Rose, Locke or Braun – were ever found or tried.

Kreisleiter Gerhard Thiele, the man chiefly responsible for the murder action, was never apprehended. Thiele fled from Gardelegen at 1800 on April 14. The day before, Major Stobbe, the chief of the local Wehrmeldeamt (recruiting office), had provided him with a Wehrmacht identity card and paybook with false personalia. Thiele was last seen saying goodbye to his wife outside his home on Stendaler Strasse 89 and wearing a civilian suit instead of his usual Party costume. His wife was interrogated, but disclosed

The sign put up by the 102nd Division at the entrance to the cemetery. (Gedenkstätte Gardelegen)

In 1953, the massacre site was made an official memorial by the East German authorities, one section of the barn wall being preserved. Text and sculpture were added later. (Karel Margry)

nothing (she lived in the GDR until her death). Persistent rumours that Thiele had found refuge in the Western Zones, later the German Federal Republic, led prosecution offices in both East and West to begin investigations into his case in the 1960s, none of them with any official result. Only in 1997, after

Five Polish survivors of Gardelegen during a visit to the cemetery on April 13, 1965, the 20th commemoration of the massacre. L-R: Tadeusz Moderski, who evaded during the march from Mieste to Gardelegen, thus escaping the massacre; Edward Antoniak, who reputedly escaped from the barn after climbing up into the rafters; Witold Modzelewski, another escapee from the barn; Josef Pamuta, one of the prisoners who volunteered to act as armed guard during the massacre (as there had been no evidence that Pamuta had actually killed anyone, no charges had been brought against him in 1945. When he showed up in Gardelegen in 1965, nothing of all this was known locally, and Pamuta was able to pose and get fêted as a survivor from inside the barn. Antoniak, who introduced him, must have known the truth but, for some reason, chose to say nothing); and Franek Krawczyk, who escaped at Letzlingen. (Gedenkstätte Gardelegen)

reunification, was the Sachsen-Anhalt criminal police finally able to confirm the rumours. Thiele had been in the West since 1947, living under the false name of Gerhard Lindemann in Düsseldorf from 1951 until his death as an 85-year-old pensioner on June 30, 1994.

Despite East-West relations deteriorating into the Cold War, work brigades of local firms and factories kept the cemetery at Gardelegen in perfect order. This practice continued after Gardelegen became part of East Germany in 1948. In September that year, the remains of 34 dead of French nationality were exhumed and transferred to the French National Cemetery at Tegel in the French sector of Berlin. (When this cemetery was dissolved in 1951-52, most of the 34 were repatriated to France.)

With the scarcity of building materials in the immediate post-war years,

The American sign erected at the cemetery in 1945 was removed by the East German authorities in 1965 and unceremoniously re-used as part of the wall of a shed in the communal cemetery, something which few people outside the cemetery workers knew. It was only after this picture, taken illegally by a young East German, Karl-Heinz Reuschel, reached the US in 1988 and was published there – and then brought to the notice of the East German authorities by their embassy – that action was undertaken. Fearing an international uproar, the GDR authorities ordered that the sign be replaced at the cemetery but when it was extracted it was found to have badly deteriorated. The original was put in store at the town museum while the authorities ordered a replica to be made. However, wood and paint had to be allocated and the fall of the GDR came before the duplicate was ready. (Karl-Heinz Reuschel)

bricks and tiles from the burned-out Isenschnibbe barn were carried off to be re-used elsewhere. In 1950, work began to turn what remained of the building into a memorial. Part of its front wall was renovated, a text added to it, and bushes were planted. The new memorial, formally dedicated in April 1953, became a venue for Party and State ceremonies. A permanent exhibition on its historical background was opened in the Gardelegen town museum in 1963. In 1965, as an additional reminder of what had happened in the region, the routes of the death marches to Gardelegen were indicated by stone markers. That same year – as a gesture of political protest against the US involvement in the Vietnam War – the big sign erected by the Americans at the cemetery was taken down.

In 1970, the status of the massacre memorial was raised to that of a regional Mahn- und Gedenkstätte (Remembrance and Memorial Site). It was re-landscaped according to the strict guidelines laid out for all East German memorials, with flag-poles, flaming urns and a speaker platform. A bronze

The replacement was finally put up in 1990. (Karel Margry)

sculpture by Jochen Sendler was added in 1971. Even more than before, the site became a place for state-organised, anti-Fascist mass meetings.

All this ended with the demise of the GDR in 1989. One surprise after reunification was the discovery of the original sign put up at the cemetery

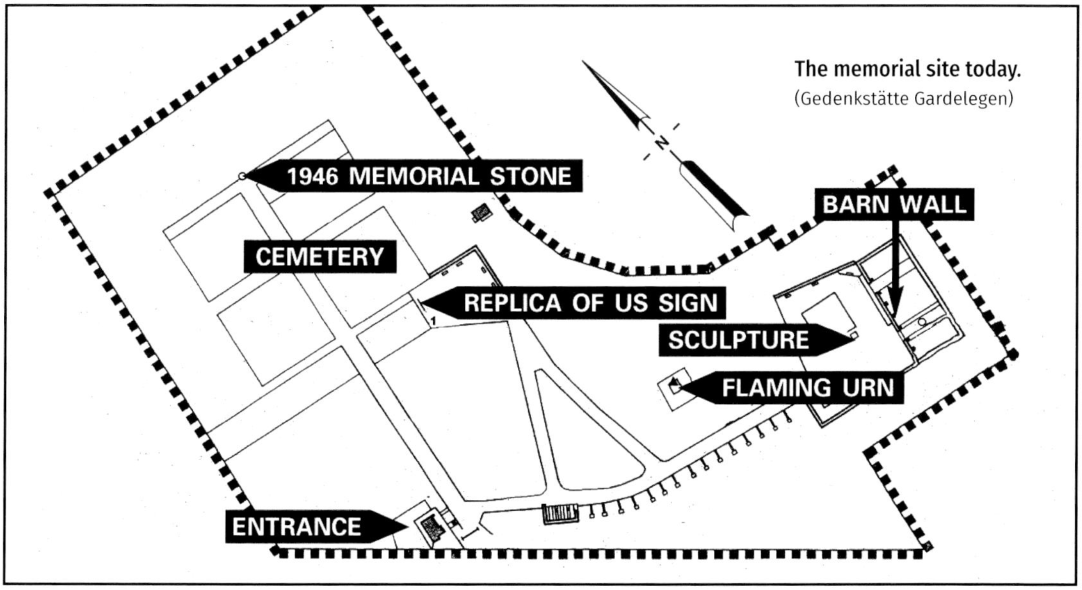

The memorial site today. (Gedenkstätte Gardelegen)

Another GDR legacy: stone markers still mark the route of the main death march from Mieste to Gardelegen via Zichtau. The red triangle was worn by political prisoners in Nazi concentration camps.
(Karel Margry)

by the Americans. After it was taken down in 1965, it had been stored away at the town cemetery. It was later used as a side wall of an open tool shed and so survived through the years. When a secretly-taken picture of it surfaced in the West in 1988, the GDR authorities, fearing a scandal, ordered it to be re-erected. However, the sign was in poor condition, so plans were made to replace it with a replica instead. Reunification came before this materialised

On April 13, 2000 – the 55th commemoration of the massacre – a delegation of veterans of the 102nd 'Ozark' Division presented a bronze plaque 'to the citizens of Gardelegen who have observed and supported General Keating's directive of 1945'. The plaque text continues: 'May this memorial be a "cry for freedom and peace" by the victims of this massacre, their homelands and our two countries'. L-R: Frau Hannelore von Baehr, mayoress of Gardelegen; Sylvia Henk, interpreter; Ernest Smith and Jim Hansen, presenting the plaque on behalf of the Ozark veterans. Jim Hansen was the lieutenant leading the patrol which first discovered the barn on April 15, 1945.
(Gedenkstätte Gardelegen)

and the replica was not finally erected near the original spot until 1990. The original sign is now on display at the Gardelegen Memorial museum.

After 1989 the Gardelegen Memorial, like the other sites dedicated to the memory of victims of Nazism in former East Germany, worked to correct the one-sided political slant of the information available to visitors. In 1991, the exhibition in the town museum was closed. New information tables were erected at the memorial itself in 1995, but plans for a dedicated museum

The new Dokumentationszentrum, opened at the site in 2020. It is located immediately to the left of the 'entrance' patch in the plan on page 163. (Gedenkstätte Gardelegen)

and visitor's centre on the site took many years to materialise. Finally, in 2020 – 75 years after the event – a newly-built Dokumentationszentrum (documentation centre) was opened there, the official dedication being done by the German Federal President, Frank-Walter Steinmeier, and the Prime Minister of the province of Sachsen-Anhalt, Dr Reiner Haseloff. The building houses a permanent exhibition and has space for temporary exhibitions, public meetings and seminars. The museum staff offers guided group tours, guidance in educational projects, and carries out scholarly research. A new museum catalogue was published in 2022.